THE
MASTER'S
CALL

THE MASTER'S CALL

A Family's Discovery of
the Way, the Truth and the Life

Athena D'Souza

Authentic™

HYDERABAD

The Master's Call
by Athena D'Souza

Copyright © 2008 by Athena D'Souza

First edition 2008
Revised edition 2008
Four reprint 2009 - 2013
Reprint 2014

ISBN: 978-81-7362-832-0

Scripture quotations used in this work are taken from the *New King James Version* (NKJV), *New International Version* (NIV) of the Bible.

Publisher's Note: The doctrinal, ideological, religious and sociological views expressed by the author in this publication may not necessarily reflect those of the publisher.

Published by
Authentic Books
Logos Bhavan, Suchitra Junction, Secunderabad 500 067, Telangana.
www.authenticindia.in

Authentic Books is an imprint of Authentic Media (India), the publishing division of OM Books Foundation.

Printed and bound in India by
Authentic Media, Secunderabad 500 067

This book is dedicated to our precious children, Maheen and Awaiz Mirza and Gulrez and Faiyaz Ally; for the emotional, intellectual and social trauma they had to endure on account of our new found faith.

Thank you for your silent support Maheen, and for showing so much sensitivity and gentleness throughout.

Thank you, Awaiz, for standing with us even when times were very rough and tough for you.

Thank you, Gulrez, for your sweet understanding and quiet acceptance of situations beyond your control.

Thank you, Faiyaz, the beloved of us all.

Ilyas and Safia Mirza,

Vizarath and Lateef Ally.

Contents

Acknowledgments

My grateful thanks first and foremost to the one this book exalts, Jesus Christ, Light of the world. If it wasn't for the Lord Jesus and his wonderful deeds, I would have nothing to write about. Thank you Lord, for your enabling and your anointing. I love you and honor your holy name.

Thanks also to Sanford, my precious husband and father of our four wonderful children, for his confidence in my abilities and gifting. You've always had more faith in me than I've had in myself. Thank you for all you've been, and all you've done for me, these past so many years of our togetherness.

I am also indebted to my Pastor—Yang Tuck Yoong for his spiritual covering over my life. If I could be half as zealous and jealous for the Lord as he is, I would be content with my lot. Thank you for your encouragement and your prayers Pastor Yang. We love you and are blessed by your love for the Lord Jesus.

Mom and dad, thank you for your love and support to me all these years and for being there whenever I needed you. I pray you'll be blessed and encouraged by these stories of Jesus' grace and goodness.

My grateful thanks and love also to my dear sisters in the Lord who have prayed for the completion of this book, namely, Mary Schrag, Loo Bee Yan, Janet Wakefield and Zeldine Reddy.

And last, but not least, to the precious couples whose testimonies I have attempted to articulate in print; thank you for making me a part of your lives and allowing me this privilege of sharing the most glorious milestone of your life with the rest of the world.

To God be all the glory.
Athena D'Souza,
Dec. 2007.

Foreword

One of the blessings I was privileged to enjoy, was meeting the Mirza and Ally families in Hyderabad, India.

I retired as Director from the Henry Martyn Institute of Islamic studies, Hyderabad, in October 1990. When the time came for me to retire, I moved from my official apartment with a heavy heart, as I had dozens of Muslim friends who lived in the same locality, and we had formed strong bonds of friendship over the years.

I moved into a flat located in Secunderabad with my family without knowing that a pleasant surprise awaited me—our meeting with the Mirza and Ally families who had their own beautiful home just across the street. Ilyas Mirza, his wife Safia, along with her brother Vizarath Ally and his wife Lateef soon became good friends of our family.

I recall many pleasant evenings spent together in their company. The discussions, meals and fellowship we shared are memories that are very precious to us. Soon Ilyas and Safia became Ilyas *Bhai* (brother) and Safia *Apa* (sister) to all of us.

The story of these two families' travel from Islam to Jesus Christ made a great impact on me and on several occasions I suggested they write their story and print it for others to share in this great testimony. I made the same request to Vizarath and his wife Lateef. At that time they were hesitant but promised to pray about it and seek God's will.

After several years, in the month of January 2007, I was informed that both families were writing their testimonies in a book and my joy knew no bounds. When I was approached and asked if I would be willing to write the foreword, I agreed, but with some hesitation due to my old age. However, taking it as a matter of great honour and privilege, I gave my word to do the needful. The story of the Mirza family is a witness, through their life and work, that they were led by the Holy Spirit to come to the Lord and Savior Jesus Christ.

I have not as yet come across any Muslim who has confessed that he or she accepted Jesus Christ because some Christians were able to explain the Sonship of Christ, or the Atonement, or the Christian dogma of the Trinity to him. It is always the Muslim's own seeking desire which compels him to read the Bible, and once he reads the gripping account of the life of our Lord, his pride is broken and his heart becomes restless to find solace in the Prince of Peace. Muslims are also moved when a small deed of brotherly love is performed by a Christian.

Let me tell you some other things of interest about each member of this wonderful family. Most readers of this book of testimonies will realize that Safia Mirza was a college lecturer, her husband Ilyas Mirza worked as Manager in a bank, but in spite of their secular jobs they chose to serve the Lord.

Safia is a forceful preacher in English and Urdu; her ministry takes her to all parts of the world as God calls her to. Her husband Ilyas loves to speak good Urdu with a Lucknow or Delhi accent.

I always enjoy his company and his logical arguments to prove his point.

In our various family gatherings we discussed the matter of starting a prayer fellowship involving our families and other friends. The fellowship went on for some time and then took the form of a small church. We wanted to give this church a suitable name and after much discussion and prayer we selected the name Bait al Noor—the House of Light.

Vizarath and Lateef are both Urdu speaking people; they love to express themselves in this sweet language. I always enjoy listening to Vizarath's Urdu sermons. He uses simple language which the church members can easily understand. Vizarath is able to expound the deep thoughts of the Bible in simple Urdu. His teacher has been the Bible. His personal study of the Bible has given him the kind of knowledge and wisdom that even seminary graduates lack.

Vizarath also runs a radio program which proclaims the gospel message. His voice is used by the Holy Spirit to carry the Word of truth to hundreds and thousands of listeners on the radio. Lateef is not only a good home-maker but a prayer warrior as well. She has acquired a wonderful knowledge of the Bible by reading her own Urdu Bible and spending several hours in devotion and meditation.

I am convinced that the story of these two families will be a blessing and inspiration to others, as it has been to me. It is an encouragement to those who belong to the same background; it is proof that the Holy Spirit is active on earth even today to bear witness to Christ.

Dr. Samuel V. Bhajjan,
Urdu Bible Translation Coordinator,
International Bible Society (South Asia).

Introduction

Conversion is the ultimate act of trauma. Whether the switch is to another religion or to another life-style, it normally leaves in its wake a string of bruised and distressed relationships and invokes a response of disdain and scorn from others. Questions, assumptions, allegations and emotional blackmail are part and parcel of the reaction towards the disloyal person who has dared to turn aside from the tradition of his/her father's religion, and chase after alien gods.

In the following pages you will read about the conversion experiences of four members of a Muslim household living in the historical city of Hyderabad. The one certain, expected recompense was death, which is the accepted fate of an infidel or *kafir*, yet that did not deter them from responding to the call of the Master and following him all the way to the cross.

When God reached down from heaven and revealed himself to them through various signs and wonders, he did it as someone completely antithetical to what they had been taught and believed in all their lives. But the undeniable evidence of his reality and love was impossible to ignore. In the end they could do nothing other than lay themselves as living sacrifices on the altar of surrender and service.

I pray that as you read these four simple stories about four simple people related by birth and marriage, you will be awed and amazed by the grace and goodness of the God who called them and drew them to his side; first to forgive and cleanse them of their sins, thus assuring them of a place with him in eternity; then in commissioning them to go forth with his glorious message of hope and love and salvation.

In John 10:14-16, 27, 28 Jesus said,

"I am the good shepherd; and I know My sheep, and am known by My own. As the Father knows Me, even so I know the Father; and I lay down My life for the sheep. And other sheep I have which are not of this fold; them also I must bring, and they will hear My voice, and there will be one flock and one shepherd. My sheep hear My voice, and I know them, and they follow Me. And I give them eternal life, and they shall never perish; neither shall anyone snatch them out of My hand."

These are the testimonies of how he did precisely that. Four members of a family who were separated by betrayal and hurt; now part of that one flock, being led by the good shepherd and living the eternal life that Jesus came to give.

Praise the Lord!

Athena D'Souza

1

$\mathscr{P}$ower in the Blood
Safia's Testimony

Crackling tension gripped the city of Hyderabad in the September of 1948 as the Nizam's forces locked horns with the Indian military in a brazen show of defiance. This showdown had been precipitated by the Nizam's desire to acquire a special Dominion Status for the Princely State of Hyderabad. Though the majority of his Hindu populace was in favor of joining with India, the Nizam and his Muslim elite were avidly anti-merger and were intent on taking their proposal all the way to the Security Council of the United Nations.

But the continued violence by the *Razakars* (the Palace's storm-troopers), ultimately forced the hand of the Central Government to send orders to the Indian National Army to sort out the issue once and for all.

In turn, the Army launched a five-pronged police action; curfew was clamped all over the city and anxious homes hastened to keep their doors firmly shut. The monsoon lightning splintering the dense, rain-filled skies only reflected the political turmoil prevalent on the ground.

It was in this scenario that my mother suddenly went into labor with her third child—me. Her earlier pregnancies had been relatively easy, but this time around the whole situation was being complicated by the fact that she would have to deliver the baby at home. It was dangerous and foolhardy to venture outdoors and she desperately wished her husband could have been by her side as she contemplated what to do. My father was a traveling salesman with the Vazir Sultan Tobacco Company and was absent from home more often than not, leaving the raising of the children to my mother. She was an uncomplaining and dutiful housewife, the epitome of gentle patience, but this was one time her husband's absence and support were desperately missed.

Breaching curfew had its own risks, but expecting a midwife to come out in this stormy weather seemed foolishly optimistic as well. The only recourse was for my mother to lean on the mercy of Allah, who is Ar-Rahim, the merciful, and pray that the one man present in the house at that time, my father's brother-in-law, would be successful in bringing home a midwife to help her out in her pain and anguish.

As her contractions took on a steadier rhythm, squeezing out the new life within her in waves of unbearable agony, my uncle rushed out in the rain to frantically search for medical help. He finally returned with a sympathetic local medical practitioner and not a minute too soon either. At exactly 10 p.m, while the Nizam of Hyderabad was struggling with the decision of surrendering his power to the forces surrounding his palace, I was safely surrendered into the waiting arms of my mother. Neither the frenzied weather, nor the political upheaval could hinder my entrance into this world.

It was the inscrutable, decisive and merciful will of Allah. And as has been done in past centuries—the *adhaan*—the first words spoken into every Muslim baby's ears, was whispered into mine by my uncle: "God is great. There is no god but Allah. Muhammad is the messenger of Allah."

This powerful declaration deposited deep in the tender receptive spirit of a new-born babe is instrumental in sowing the first seeds for a harvest of fierce devotion and love towards Allah and his messenger. It is the bedrock, the foundation of our faith, and the first step in training us to love our religion, to be proud of it and to honor and revere our Prophet like no other. To me, as to the rest of the Muslims, the Prophet Muhammad was Insaan-e-Kamil, the perfect man.

Childhood

My parents decided to name me Safia; the pure and wise one. We were a typical Muslim household that thronged the streets of Hyderabad in the early 1950s. There was nothing unusual about us, nothing that would make us stand out from the rest of our community. As was the norm those days, we lived with the rest of our extended family in a big bungalow on an avenue lined with shady trees. Motor traffic was not frenetic and homicidal like it is now, and walking to our destination was a course of pleasure, not cause for a heart attack. When I was a little child, the streets were so open and inviting, we could play on them safely without any fear of being run over, and when the vendors rolled their carts to our front gates, I would be the first to run out and prod the vegetables and fruits for firm freshness and to bargain for good prices. Life was simple and uncomplicated.

My childhood memories are happy ones. Living in an extended family filled with noisy, happy-go-lucky cousins and siblings was heaven for me. We were 13 children and 8 adults all together, and to coexist peacefully, we had to develop a spirit of tolerance towards each other; there was no other alternative. Other than that, we also rested secure in the fact that our parents nurtured us spiritually as well as physically. My mother hired a religious teacher, an *ustad*, who came home thrice a week to teach us Arabic so that we could be proficient in our holy scriptures. It was a discipline that was inculcated early in life and left an indelible mark on our world view. Arabic is not our mother tongue, more so the classical Arabic of the 7th century A.D. in which the Koran is written, and it is not an easy language to master, but we learnt it because we loved Allah and Islam, which we believed was the religion that superseded all other religions.

I am blessed with a sharp memory and good learning skills so it was just a matter of time before I could read and recite the whole Koran. I was nine years old when I completed reading the Koran from cover to cover for the first time, and it was a day of great celebration in the family. My mother honored the *ustad* with sweets, a good meal, and a *hadiya*, which was a special gift for the teacher. I was garlanded and wore the prettiest clothes I had at that time. My teacher and parents were extremely proud of this religious accomplishment.

For my secular education, I was admitted to a reputed Catholic Institution, St. Ann's High School, at the tender age of three. A few years down the line I received a double promotion in class. This resulted in me appearing for my Senior Cambridge examination at a very young age, and on my early graduation I had to make important decisions regarding the direction of my further education and career options.

My mother was not comfortable with sending me to work in an office where there were men, so my choices were narrowed even further. However, I had discovered a love for teaching early in my life, and so I enrolled in the Teachers' Training Institute. There too I was the youngest trainee in my cohort.

After graduating as a full-fledged teacher, I applied for a job in my Alma Mater since it was an All Girls' school where even the management was run by women. I had majored in History because of my keen interest in gleaning life-lessons from the past. My excellent memory for remembering dates and deeds helped tremendously, and I soon became aware that my passion for this subject and my ability to make it come alive for my students quickly earned me the reputation of being a formidably good teacher. I was proud of that recognition.

Marital Bliss

Soon it was time for my parents to arrange my marriage to a respectable Muslim man, and they found the perfect match in Ilyas. Ilyas belonged to a distinguished and reputed family from old Hyderabad. He was quite the catch of the day—tall, debonair and handsome. I liked him the moment I set eyes on him in a mixed gathering of relatives, but I could not decide whether I wanted to get married and lose my new-found independence. The deciding factor ultimately was the element of disgrace our culture placed on having an unmarried daughter in the house. That was something I did not want to subject my parents to as I was almost 25 years old by then, with a swiftly diminishing rate of matrimonial eligibility. So I allowed myself to flow in the stream of excitement generated by my friends and family, and participated with some enthusiasm in all the frenzied shopping for brocade saris and intricate jewellery.

The *nikaah* (solemnizing) ceremony and all the celebrations finally came to a successful end on a warm summer evening after much feasting and merriment. Lavish compliments on my beautiful bridal finery and the grand jewellery I was wearing faded out as everyone returned to their homes satiated with food and drink.

It was then that the stark realization of what had just transpired hit me between my eyes. Life, as I had known it all these years, had finally come to an end, and I was on the brink of a new era with a man I didn't know, and a family I had to adopt and treat as my own. Countless brides who are reading this will empathize with what I'm talking about; the trepidation, the muted excitement and all the other indescribable emotions that go coursing through one's heart at that precise moment of destiny.

However, I need not have worried. My husband turned out to be a gentle and noble-hearted man who loved, respected and treated me with grace, and I blessed Allah for giving me a good life partner. In a short while there was an addition to our family—a beautiful little girl whom we both cherished and who filled our lives with joy and laughter.

Professional Satisfaction

Even though I now had a family to take care of, my professional life had not been put on hold. I still continued to teach History, Religion and Culture at the nearby Convent School and enjoyed every minute of it. Teaching was my joy and passion and I could not see myself working at home all day. Nothing wrong with that, but I saw no need to discontinue with teaching and considered myself perfectly capable of fulfilling both responsibilities at home and at work equally well. Thank God I had a like-minded husband who gave me the leeway to follow my heart's desire.

My supreme confidence in my abilities and capabilities made me a force to be reckoned with in the School Staff Room and my opinions were considered weighty and wise, even though I was the youngest teacher there. I also had a reputation for being sharp, quick-witted and the kind of woman not to be trifled with; yet, I was hugely popular because of my ability to tell jokes and use satire to my advantage. Perhaps it was the incongruity of anything funny emerging from such a serious, deadpan face that took people by surprise and caused them dissolve in laughter. I don't know what it was, but I had the ability to make people either laugh or tremble before me. It was quite a power trip in my opinion!

In 1976, there was an addition to our school ranks. A Christian lady named Madhubala joined as a teacher and I gradually began noticing a slight shift in the power alignment in the Staff Room. Even though it wasn't anything she did deliberately, I sensed this newcomer was stealing my thunder in some way. Whereas, before, I was the only one whose advice and opinion was sought after, now Madhubala's viewpoint was solicited and equated with mine.

I began to feel a slight waning in my authority and influence as colleagues started going to her for counsel and advice, side-tracking me smoothly in the process. It irked me initially, so I began to observe her carefully to see what was so special about her technique. She seemed to listen attentively to their problems before giving them her counsel, just like I did, but then, and this was incredible, she topped it off by praying for them, which I never could have done. I noticed that the recipients of her prayers left her side looking decidedly calmer and happier.

There was something about Madhubala that prompted a spontaneous affection in me towards her. Jealousy would have been a more appropriate emotion, since she seemed to be usurping my throne in the Staff Room, but she overflowed with such a peculiar love and compassion that it was impossible to bear her any ill-will.

Jesus Introduced

The one mistake that she did make, however, was to try and talk to me about Jesus Christ. She asked me, "Do you believe in Jesus Christ?"

I answered her, "Yes, of course I believe."

She then asked, "But what do you believe about him?"

I replied, "I believe he is a prophet of God."

"No, no, you must believe that he is the Son of God," was her quick and firm response.

The way she referred to him as the Son of God made me see red and set a siren off in my head and heart. It was absolutely ridiculous! How could anyone claim to be the Son of God? The very idea was sacrilegious and blasphemous to my soul. How, in the name of everything that is holy, could God produce a son through a woman? It was unthinkable.

To my Muslim mind, Christianity was an inferior religion for precisely this reason. Christians were deluded, deceived and misled people who had faith in a corrupted Bible and could actually believe that God would reproduce himself through an ordinary woman. And if that wasn't enough, they put her on par with the Almighty and referred to her as the mother of God! The whole scenario filled me with complete distaste and I told Madhubala in no uncertain terms to not even start trying to explain something so nauseating to me. I told her, "Let us be friends, but let us leave Jesus Christ out of our friendship."

When she saw that she was making no headway with me and that our discussions were ending up in heated arguments, she decided to do something far more effective instead. She retreated from the battle lines and turned to divine reinforcement for help. So, every afternoon during lunch, she closeted herself in an empty classroom and began to pray for me. Nobody knew what she was doing; we were all too busy indulging in our own self-absorbed gossip sessions to bother about anyone else.

But Madhubala, with a divine mandate and burden on her heart, sacrificed her lunch break every day to pray devotedly and persistently for me. What did she pray for? Only she and

God knew. Perhaps she pleaded with the Almighty to open my eyes to the truth and to protect me from my own arrogance and pride; perhaps she prayed for the Will of God to be established in my life. I don't know, but what I do know is that, after two years of sacrificial praying, God answered her prayer in a very dramatic manner.

I want to pause here and insert something important. Never, ever, underestimate the power of effective and sacrificial intercession. The power of prayer can never be understated. It required just one obedient woman pursuing God with a burden which he himself put on her heart, to change the atmosphere of her workplace and the eternal destiny of her colleague.

The Retreat

In 1978, Sister Margaret Mary, the Principal of my school happened to attend a Charismatic Retreat in Mumbai and it was there that she was introduced to the biblical doctrine of spiritual rebirth; the necessity of being born again, as directed by Jesus in the Gospel of John. That experience changed her life completely and she returned to school a transformed and enthused person, full of fiery zeal and passion.

Sister Margaret Mary then decided it would be quite selfish of her to keep this knowledge and blessing to herself and not give her staff an opportunity to hear and experience these truths. So she made an announcement. The school would be shut down for three days, during which every member of her staff would be required to attend a Spiritual Retreat. Father D'Souza was invited to come down from Mumbai to conduct it, the dates were set and all the arrangements were finalized.

Well, none of us teachers minded this kind of spiritual coercion at all. I had already lined up all my Romance novels to read on the sly during the lectures, and I'm sure the other teachers had also prepared their own side-activities to indulge in while feigning interest in the lectures. As far as I was concerned, this was going to be a relaxed and paid vacation for me.

Little did I know what plans God had for that "paid vacation"! The first day of the retreat dawned bright and clear, and after we had all settled down, Father D'Souza began the proceedings with an explosive introduction.

"Which guru or religious leader or even god has said, I have come that you might have life and life more abundantly? Which religious leader, which so-called prophet, which guru, which teacher, which god has ever said, 'I have come so that your sins may be forgiven?' Did anyone take our sins upon himself? Did anyone take responsibility for our sins? Did Ram do so? Did Krishna? Did Buddha? Did Muhammad?"

The unexpected inclusion of my Prophet's name jerked me up instantly and I felt my face begin to turn red hot. This priest could talk about any other religion, I didn't care. He could talk about any other religious leader, I was not bothered. But he dared not talk about my Prophet in the same breath as with the others; he had absolutely no right to do that.

I slowly began to seethe with rage and it took all of my self control not to walk out of the hall. The rest of the morning session passed by in a sullen haze, and when we broke for a short recess, I went to the Staff Room deliberating within myself whether I should go or stay. After calming down a bit, I decided to give him one more chance to redeem himself, but resolved that if he offended me again, I would pack up and go home, even if it meant a loss of pay.

So I returned for the next session, still in quite a huff, but Fr. D'Souza seemed bent on continuing with his provocative questioning.

"Who are you?" he asked, looking around at the faces before

him. One teacher stood up and said, "I'm a Math teacher," another stood up and said, "I'm a Hindu," another replied, "I'm a clerk."

After listening to ten such introductions, the priest shook his head and remarked, "No, that is what you all are in your own opinion. As human beings, we tend to identify and separate ourselves according to our faith, our profession, our race, our colour, our creed, our nationality. But when God looks at us, he doesn't see us as a housewife or a clerk or a teacher." Then he paused and pointed his finger towards us and declared, "When God looks at us, he brands the whole lot of us in one category— WE ARE ALL SINNERS!"

And with that dramatic announcement, he paused and sat down to let his words sink in.

Then he stood up and proceeded to list out all our sins. There was no mention of adultery or murder or anything horrible like that—he knew that we were all morally upright citizens. Instead he began pointing out innocuous practices like going late for work and fabricating a lame excuse, or signing the roster for our absent friends and covering up with little white lies. What about the kind of books we read? I immediately thought of the book in my bag. Or the movies we watched—we had planned to go and watch a popular movie later. Or the language we used—I cringed as I thought of our colourful lingo, especially when we gossiped about others.

I began to feel the warmth of conviction begin creeping under my skin now. "We are all sinners," he reiterated, "all sinners," and he continued to list out some more of what I considered as minor misdemeanors, but which he regarded as sins.

As I listened to him, that warmth began to slowly travel upwards and flush my cheeks till my face felt like it was on fire. It was an extremely uncomfortable sensation, but more than that, was this strange overpowering conviction that was flooding my soul. There were so many other teachers with me in that room, but I began to feel like he was referring to me only, and was revealing all the secrets of my life only, and by the end of that session I was plagued with only one question in my heart, "WHO had gone and told him about ME?"

I returned to the Staff Room during the next break and sat pensively in a corner, mulling over all that I had just heard. Before today, no one could have convinced me that I was not a good person; in fact, I placed myself in the same bracket that all morally upright, decent, respectable and virtuous people belonged in. Now suddenly, I wasn't too sure any more.

This time, I spoke to nobody. I could no longer raise my voice and shout about going home on loss of pay. I began to feel an unfamiliar guilt over my sins so overwhelm me, that I became as quiet as a mouse. While the other staff members were still talking around the table I went away to a corner of the room. I felt very uncomfortable. Perhaps there was something to what he was saying. I decided the best thing would be to clear things up with Allah himself, so I simply said, "God, I don't want to do those sins any more. I just want to be a better person."

Having straightened that out with God and feeling a load lift off my back, I returned for the third session in a calmer and more serene mood. This session now focussed on the fact that if we acknowledged and agreed with the fact that all men are sinners; it stood to reason that all men needed a savior to save them from their sins. Would God be so whimsical as to condemn us in our sinfulness and make no provision for our deliverance? What would constitute our salvation? Good works? Charity? Kindness? Monasticism? I waited keenly for his answer, but Fr. D'Souza suddenly changed tack and veered off into an announcement and an invitation, "I will be conducting a prayer meeting at the chapel this evening. How many of you would like to attend it?" No one was more surprised than I when my hand seemed to shoot up of its own accord. Short, sharp intakes of breath and a stunned silence followed, as my friends absorbed this phenomenon—Safia, wanting to go to a prayer meeting! Stupefied disbelief then gave way to fiercely whispered comments which shot out like a barrage of bullets. "Stop trying to impress him Safia...Why are you lying through your teeth Safia?...Don't bluff him...Who are you trying to impress...?" and finally the topping on the cake, "This year she's a Catholic, next year she'll be a nun. . . !"

I laughed along with my friends, knowing that if I was in their place, I would have reacted in exactly the same way. But on my way home that evening, I suddenly remembered that we were in the month of Ramadan and I would have to be at home to serve my husband his *iftar*, (breaking-fast meal). Ilyas was a practicing, conservative Muslim who fasted religiously every year, and it was my duty as his wife to prepare his meal and serve it to him. So it didn't seem possible that I would be able to attend the meeting after all. Then a thought occurred to me to ask God if he wanted me to go, so I told him, "Allah, if you want me to be at that meeting tonight for some special reason, I know you will take me there."

With that said I went home, prepared the food, and while my husband was eating, I casually remarked to him, "There is a prayer meeting in the chapel at 7 p.m. tonight. Do you think I should go?" Without missing a bite, and with his mouth full of food, he replied, "What are you waiting here for? You go and I'll pick you up when it's over."

This was incredible. In the past, I had often overheard Christian wives complaining of how Christian husbands would not allow their Christian wives to go to Christian prayer meetings. But here was a Muslim man, allowing his Muslim wife to go to a Christian prayer meeting—and even offering to bring her home. It was ironic. And then the words that I had spoken to God earlier came back to remind me: "If you want me to be at that meeting for a special reason, you will take me there." Instantly, and for no logical reason, my heart was filled with an anticipation I had never experienced before. I could barely contain myself as I rushed down to the school chapel.

Heavenly Encounter

As I entered the crowded chapel, I looked around for some familiar faces of friends, but not finding any, I sat down in the first available space on the floor. The place was packed with worshipers already deep in fervent prayer and worship, and as I adjusted my senses to the devotion permeating the room, I began to sense a tangible presence of something divine gently suffusing the atmosphere. There was deep adoration radiating from the worshipers, and the music and lyrics of the song they were singing began to stir my heart. A sweet and glorious presence, like a silken sheet began to rest softly on my soul.

When I had come into the chapel that evening, there were two Christian truths I was completely ignorant of. The first was that Jesus Christ had the power to forgive sins and second, that this forgiveness was made possible only by his shed blood on the cross. Ignorant of any and every Christian dogma, doctrine or creed, I just sat expectantly on that floor, waiting for God to do something special for me.

As I waited quietly and reverently in that worship-saturated ambience, suddenly something very strange began to occur. My eyes were open, yet superimposed on my natural vision, I began to see large, crystal-clear images of my life begin to unfold like a movie. It was a streaming collage of my existence, but what stood out in sharp clarity were all the offences I had ever committed against God. Every sin, every fault of mine was exposed in stark reality. It was a horrible and shattering picture and I felt a deep pain in my heart as I began to weep in grief and remorse.

As my tears collected in the palm of my hands, I heard Fr. D'Souza's voice gently encourage the congregation, "If anyone feels prompted to pray, this would be a good time to do so. The Lord is here to listen to your prayer." I did not really know how to pray spontaneously; we were taught to memorize scripted prayers; so I was completely shocked when I suddenly found myself pleading loudly with God to forgive me for all the sins he had just revealed to me!

Hardly had those words left my mouth when I was suddenly transported to the most beautiful spiritual experience of my life. My physical body went numb and heavy, but something from inside of me was wrenched out sharply and I began to have a dual experience. It was an out-of-body experience in which I could turn back and see my body sitting on the floor; but in my spirit I began to float high, through the ceiling, out into the open sky, and as I rose and my head touched the first thick cloud, it seemed like someone pulled me above it, and switched on all the lights!

I was bathed in rays and rays of stunning, blinding light. It was a rapturous, euphoric moment! There was brilliant brightness all around me and I thought I had reached the seventh heaven. It is very hard to describe such a rare and exquisite experience in words except to say that I was soaked in joy and love and warmth—but it was overwhelming and almost too much to bear, so I cried out to God, "Enough God, enough," still meaning Allah and immediately I felt myself descend in my spirit.

As my body and my spirit were once again united in the

chapel, I gradually became aware of my surroundings and the chorus that was being sung echoed clearly in my ears. It seemed to be about someone's blood. "There is power, there is power, there is wonder-working power, in the blood of the Lamb." I reluctantly opened my eyes from that blissful experience, still basking in the remnants of its ecstasy, and tried to focus on the song, and it was then that I noticed a bright red blob on my right thumb. It looked suspiciously like blood, but it couldn't have been. I hadn't cut myself; I hadn't even jammed my thumb that would have made it black and blue. This red blob wasn't oozing, it wasn't flowing; it was as though someone had just taken an ink-filler and squeezed a drop of red ink onto a blotting paper. Strange as it was, I ignored it for the time being, as I wanted to continue being immersed in this wonderful spiritual after-glow.

As I left the chapel to go home, I found my husband waiting for me at the school gate. He immediately inquired, "So, how was the prayer meeting?"

I replied, "Oh Ilyas, I wish you had been there! It was so good! I have decided that every time there is a prayer meeting like this one, I will attend." At the back of my mind, I thought that I would have this experience every time at a prayer meeting. How naive I was.

The Blood Drop

That night, as I began washing the cooking vessels in preparation for my husband's pre-dawn meal for the next day, I became aware of that drop of blood on my thumb again. I remembered I had seen it earlier at the chapel, so without hesitation I opened the tap to wash it off. The water gushed out forcefully, but to my surprise, the mark didn't smudge even a bit. I stared at it puzzled, and tried washing it off again. Still nothing happened. A mild panic began to overtake me so I put some concentrated detergent on it and scrubbed hard again. It still remained stark red. My panic mounted and I began trembling a bit. What was the meaning of this? Why wasn't it rubbing out? What was happening to me? Why was I trembling like this?

I continued to scrub and rub; yet it stayed on. So I stopped, leaned against the kitchen sink and took a deep breath to calm myself and to think of what to do next. The events of the evening flashed through my mind's eye, and suddenly I began to feel a sensation like electric currents passing up and down through my body, from the top of my head to the sole of my feet and back up again.

That was more than I could take. I ran into the hall where my husband was doing his mandatory reading of the Koran. All Muslims must complete the reading of the Koran during the month of Ramadan, (so we are told and taught) otherwise their fasts will not be considered meritorious by God. At that moment however I was more concerned and agitated with what was happening to me, so I interrupted my husband's religious duties and forced him to listen to my story first. I related every single detail of the evening and then flashed my thumb before his eyes. He listened to everything very calmly, then looked at me, looked at my thumb and said, "Why are you behaving like Lady Macbeth? Just relax and go to bed. I'm sure it'll be gone by the morning." Nothing on earth could ever disconcert my phlegmatic husband.

I tried to follow his advice, but I couldn't sleep one wink that night. I thought that Fr. D'Souza must have mesmerized me in some way, so I decided that the next day I would check the thumbs of all those who had been at the chapel and see if any of them had this strange mark as well. Everyone thought I had gone a bit crazy as I went around twisting their hands and staring at their thumbs, but when I checked, not a single person had any mark. My anxiety began to rise again because I realized that something supernatural was happening only to me and it was frightening.

God's Plans

I then decided to ask for an appointment with Fr. D'Souza to get some kind of an explanation from him. He met with me during one of the recesses and I told him all that had happened during the prayer meeting he had conducted. I left nothing out and showed him my thumb and the blood stain which was refusing to wash out, and told him about the electric currents that were still sweeping over me in waves. Then I asked him for an explanation. What did he think was happening to me?

He looked steadily at me for a while and then he closed his eyes in deep thought; then he looked at my thumb and then he looked at me again, and simply said, "I think God has plans for you."

"Plans?" I echoed, "What kind of plans? And why me? How can I know what those plans are? Do you know? Can you tell me?"

He looked at me gently and answered, "How can I know what plans God has for you? You will have to find it out yourself."

"How can I find it out myself and why will God speak to me?" I said. "I am not the prophet Moses that God would speak to me."

Then he picked up his Bible and said, "Do you know something? This is a talking book. God speaks to us through this book. Open it, read it, and you will hear from God."

I stared at him quite bewildered. "How can I read this Bible? There are hundreds of pages. Do you mean to say I can just ask God what plans he has for me and then open the Bible at random and the answer will be on that very page?"

"Yes," he replied, "I believe he will do it this way for you. Ask him what you need to ask and I believe that God will answer you through the pages of his written Word. For now you can find out his plans for you in this manner, but don't make it a habit."

Well, that sounded simple enough to do, so I returned home eager to put it to the test. The currents of electricity coursing through my body continued to buzz me intermittently but I was calmer now, with an eager anticipation that I would be getting some answers soon.

After serving my husband his evening meal and doing all my ritual purification like a good Muslim, I laid out my prayer mat and prepared to read the Bible. At this point I want to extend my gratitude and bless the Gideons for the wonderful work they do in distributing the Word of God. Nine years earlier they had come to our school and given each of us a Bible. We paid nothing for it. I had accepted one out of sheer politeness, but had since thrown it at the back of a shelf and forgotten about its existence. When my mother saw it with me, she warned me, "Don't read that book. The Christians have corrupted it and filled it with falsehoods."

I had faithfully complied with her wishes. But if the Gideons had not been faithful in giving us that Bible, I would not have been a Christian today.

The Mandate

As I held the Bible in my hands and began flipping through its pages randomly, I asked God, "Please tell me what plans you have for me. Please reveal them to me. I shall follow them, but please take away this blood from my thumb because I feel like a criminal."

Then I stopped flipping and looked down at the page that was spread open, and my eyes immediately fell on a paragraph written in red letters. They were the words of Jesus speaking to his disciples in verse 18 in the 28th chapter of the Gospel of Matthew.

Then Jesus came and said . . . The impact of those words hit me immediately and my focus shifted from Allah to Jesus. All along Allah was the one on whom I had been focussing. But now the spotlight suddenly shifted from Allah to Jesus because it was Jesus who was speaking. These were his words.

Jesus said, *All authority in heaven and on earth has been given to Me.* My eyes opened wide and I paused to absorb the implications of that statement. What a wonderful way to introduce himself to me. Jesus was claiming for himself such a high position. He was showing me his status in the universe. He must possess great power to have all authority in heaven and on earth. He seemed almost like Allah. Was he co-equalled with Allah then?

I continued to read the next verse, *Go, therefore and make disciples of all the nations, baptizing them in the name of the Father and of the Son and of the Holy Spirit, teaching them to observe all things that I have commanded you, and lo, I am with you always, even to the end of the age.*

I stared at these words in puzzlement. These were the plans God had for me? I read and reread the words, trying to make some sense of them. What kind of impossible plans were these?

Then I decided to speak to Jesus directly, "Jesus, how can this be your plan for me? Who and what am I? First of all, I am a woman; a Muslim woman, and a married Muslim woman at that. Do you not know all the implications involved? It won't take long for my husband to divorce me. Within three months, in the presence of two male witnesses, he will just need to say "I divorce you" once every month, and I shall be a disgraced, divorced woman. How then will I show my face to anyone? That would be a stigma I would have to carry all my life and what about my daughter— who will ever marry her then?"

"And Jesus, you want me to go to nations? How can I go to nations? I have not been to the nearest church down the road to worship and you want me to go to nations? I will need my husband's permission just to make a passport. And what can I teach about you when I don't even know my own scriptures well enough?"

"Furthermore," I continued, "Do you realize what my in-laws and my people will do to me? I will be rejected, I will be disowned, I will be ostracized, I will be persecuted, and I may even be put to death. I will be signing my own death warrant, so to say."

Deep fear began to assail me now as I imagined my fate, and I started to tremble at the prospect of this tremendous task. My heart and mind immediately rebelled. "No, I cannot do this. I will be losing everything if I attempt to do what you are asking me to do. I will lose my reputation, my husband, my child, my family, my society, my people who are so very dear to me."

"These cannot be your plans for me. I cannot teach about you. I know nothing about you. Give me some other plans and please take away this blood on my thumb. I cannot do all that you're asking, but yes, I do want you to be with me always."

I closed the Bible and looked down to check my right thumb, but the blood spot was still there. I decided I would inquire of God again the next day. After a fitful night's sleep, I repeated the same procedure as I purified and prepared myself on the prayer mat to read the Scriptures. With much trepidation and fear I once again asked God to speak to me but begged him not to give me the same plan he had given yesterday.

As I opened the Bible at random again, my eyes fell on Acts chapter 18, verse 9 and 10 where Jesus was speaking, this time to the apostle Paul. "Do not be afraid, but speak, and do not keep silent. For I am with you and no one will attack you to hurt you: for I have many people in this city."

I was stunned! This really was a talking book! Fr. D'Souza

was right. Just yesterday I had informed Jesus that I would be persecuted and attacked and that I was too afraid, and now here he was assuring me of his own personal protection. It was amazing and incredible. But what was it that he wanted me to speak about? What did he not want kept silent? I continued reading down to the end of the chapter until the latter part of verse 28 where it was written, *testify that Jesus is the Christ.*

I began to ponder silently about all this as I looked down at my right thumb again. The blood was still there, bright and unfaded. It struck me then that in the course of just three days, my whole world had been turned completely upside down.

On the final day of the retreat Fr.James asked if anyone had anything to share or any feedback to give. I stood up before the big crowd in the auditorium and testified (as in Acts 18:28) about everything that had happened to me the past two days. I didn't know what giving a testimony meant. I simply told them honestly and sincerely all that I had experienced and showed them the blood.

The reactions to my story ranged from belief to disbelief, to indifference and even to accusations of mental instability. But strangely enough, none of those reactions affected my heart which was gripped with an inexplicable joy and peace even as I experienced my first taste of rejection and scorn.

While walking home however, fresh doubts began to assail me again, and I began to wonder if all that had happened to me was simply a work of my own imagination, or worse still, a deceptive ploy of the devil? How could I be absolutely sure it was really God and not anyone else?

Appeal for Confirmation

So, I decided to put Jesus Christ to the test and I told Him, "Jesus, I am going to tell my orthodox, conservative Muslim husband that

I have decided to follow you, and you know that it is impossible for a Muslim husband to accept a woman whom he married as a Muslim, but who then turns apostate. So, if your promise for protection still stands, please prove it to me now, because you said that no man shall hurt me or harm me. When I talk to my husband, let him not hurt or divorce me but let him accept my decision amicably. I am asking you to do the impossible now so that I will have no more doubts left."

As soon as I returned home I went to my husband and dropped the bombshell, "Ilyas, there is something serious I have to tell you. All that has been happening to me thus far you are aware of. I have been struggling these past three days, unable to quite understand all that God is doing to me. But now, there is this strange assurance in my heart of joy and peace, and a prompting within to obey and follow Jesus Christ. I feel this blood on my thumb will not go until and unless I say yes to Jesus. I know this will come as a shock to you, but my mind is made up."

"You are now left with two options as far as I can see. You can either divorce me, which is the easier option, and which is fair to you after the kind of decision I have taken, or you can choose the second option; we can both agree to continue living under one roof, me as a Christian and you as a Muslim. Divorce is going to hurt us very much, especially our daughter who has brought so much joy in our lives."

"But bear in mind, if you are gracious enough to choose the second alternative, it will not be easy for you, as you will have to face much taunting from our people and your ego will be bruised. Some may throw it to your face that you were not firm enough to put your foot down regarding my turning to Jesus Christ and that may hurt you. So, now what will your decision be? "

I waited with bated breath for his reply.

As I watched his face register emotions ranging from surprise to shock to anger to uncertainty, he finally composed himself and thought silently for a long while. Then he looked at me and gave me such a noble answer. He said, "What you believe about Jesus Christ is in your heart. How can your convictions and beliefs which are in your heart change our relationship as husband and wife? We will still be husband and wife no matter what our beliefs. Come, you have gone through so much and it's been three days since you've eaten food properly. Tonight, I will serve you dinner. Come and eat." As tears began to flow from my eyes, he turned to my daughter who was sitting on his lap and told her, "Go and bring my kerchief and wipe your mother's tears."

Words can never describe the emotions I experienced at that moment. The knowledge that my family was not going to be torn apart, and that my husband was not going to hurt or reject me caused me to weep with joy and gratitude. Jesus had answered my prayer in such a marvelous manner; I was very overwhelmed and grateful.

The next morning I once again turned to the Bible and I told Jesus Christ, "Lord Jesus, I want one last word of confirmation from you to show me that you did it all, and that you spoke to my husband last night even though he didn't know it."

I opened to Matthew's Gospel, the first chapter and read from verses 18-20:

"This is how the birth of Jesus Christ came about: His mother Mary was pledged to be married to Joseph, but before they came together, she was found to be with child through the Holy Spirit. Because Joseph her husband was a righteous man and did not want to expose her to public disgrace, he had in mind to divorce her quietly. But after he had considered this, an angel of the Lord appeared to him in a dream and said, "Joseph, son of David, do not be afraid to take Mary home as your wife, because what is conceived in her is from the Holy Spirit."

I closed the Bible and thought to myself. Something precisely like this could have happened last night. My husband was a good man and he could easily have thought of setting me aside and divorcing me quietly even as Joseph had. But the Holy Spirit must have spoken to him even though he was not aware of it. I wept in gratitude once again for the protective hand of God upon my life.

Complete Surrender

I closed my eyes and then I told Jesus, "I am willing to go wherever you will take me. I am willing to teach if you will teach me first." Later on people would ask me, "Did you invite Jesus into your heart? Did you confess your sins and ask Jesus to forgive you and to come into your heart?" I could not understand what they were talking about. Some others would ask, "Did you say the sinner's prayer?"

What sinner's prayer? I have yet not found any sinner's prayer written anywhere in the Bible. If there had been one, I would have recited it. What I did that morning after I closed my Bible with weeping and thanksgiving in my heart, was the only form of the sinner's prayer that I knew; my total surrender and obedience to the will and command of Jesus Christ.

Since the past three days I had done everything humanly possible to wash off that blood mark from my thumb, but the moment I spoke those words of surrender and service, the blood spot just disappeared. It vanished instantaneously. Its purpose had been accomplished. My right thumb looked absolutely clean again.

Later in life, when people heard my story, they marveled at the miracle of how the blood had first appeared when everyone was singing the hymn, "There is power, there is power, there is wonder-working power in the blood of the Lamb," and how it disappeared the moment I agreed to Jesus' call on my life.

The greater miracle however, was that, true to his word, no one had harmed me or hurt me in any way. My people did not stone me and my in-laws did not reject me. They were more than good to me because they are such lovely people. Whatever resentment they might have had, they kept it in their hearts and there was no blatant aggression from anyone. I was preserved and kept safe by the power and promise of God's Word.

But even more, the greatest miracle was what Jesus accomplished in me; the transformation he brought about in my very soul. Paul tells us in the second letter to the Corinthians, chapter 5, verse 17, "If any man is in Christ, he is a new creation, the old is past, behold the new is come." That was certainly evident in me now. I had new attitudes, new perceptions, new revelations, new compassions and new passions. I observed that the problems didn't vanish just because the Holy Spirit was now in my heart. In fact, they grew bigger, they multiplied and even became quite complicated, but somehow I was different. The Holy Spirit gave me the wisdom and strength to face it all.

A hunger for the Word of God and for prayer and intercession began to take a hold of my spirit. Every spare moment I could find, I would run to my room to commune with Jesus. Things that had seemed important in the past seemed frivolous and superficial now. I had a mission given to me by the Lord himself—to show from the Scriptures that Jesus was the Christ and to go to the nations with this message. I needed to study and to know his Word in order to fulfill that commission.

But it was easier said than done. Even though my husband had been supportive of my conversion, I had to abide by certain conditions, the main one being that I was not allowed to go to church. I could sit at home and read my Bible, I could stay at home and pray; he would not object to that. But as for going to church to worship, that was out of the question.

So I honored his request in obedient submission, and for the next ten years I stayed at home and worshiped God by myself. It was difficult at times. To be deprived of Christian fellowship, to not be nurtured or discipled, to not be able to worship in freedom was very hard to bear. But the sustaining grace of Christ, the love of God and the fellowship of the Holy Spirit enabled me to press in and press on. There was never a day when his presence didn't surround and uplift me, not even in times of emotional drought or in seasons of despair and loss.

Three years after my conversion, a Canadian missionary couple, Henry and Amanda Poetker, came to visit me in the hospital two days after my son's birth. They had heard about me from someone else, and so they came to pray with me, to encourage me and to simply love me. I began to call them on the phone and ask questions when I was confused or discouraged and they would disciple me to the best of their ability, but that was all the help I got. However, the Holy Spirit continued to faithfully teach me and give me revelation from his Word as I studied it and hid it in my heart.

More Trials

We went through times of much trauma and upheaval. The Lord had promised his disciples that they would have tribulation in this world, and I certainly was having my fair share. Yet it couldn't have been very easy for my husband either. He had to face his friends and relations everyday knowing what they thought of him; that he was not firm enough to rein in his apostate wife and allowing her instead, an infidel, to stay under his roof. I admired and respected my husband for not giving in to social and emotional pressures and for continuing to care for us.

But this subtle, relentless pressure on our lives continued for many years, until one day, everything came to an unexpected head. My husband suddenly erupted and said, "I can't take this anymore. I think it's time we went our separate ways." After all these years, he was finally ready to give up and divorce me!

I was so upset and angry with God that I went in to my bedroom, bolted the door and banged my fists on the pillows, weeping in frustration and complaining bitterly to Jesus, "I am very disappointed in you Lord. For ten years I stayed at home and obeyed my husband by not going to church. I curtailed my own desires and gave in to his; for ten years I continued to believe that you would touch my husband, and is this the result of my sacrifices and faithfulness? Now what do you want me to do?"

The reply came swiftly and loudly. A voice in my heart clearly said, "Tomorrow, you go to church." I was convinced I had heard from God.

Sunday morning dawned and I began to get dressed to go out. My husband asked me, "Where are you going?" Out came the truth, "I am going to New Life Assembly of God Church." I opened the door and walked out. I was probably more shocked than Ilyas, as I had never done something like this before, but when I sat in the auto rickshaw, I wept all the way. "Jesus, I never wanted to go like this, all alone, to church. I really believed that both Ilyas and I would go together one day."

As I entered the Conference Hall where the New Life Assembly of God Church was meeting, the first song I heard was, "I will enter His gates with thanksgiving in my heart; I will enter His courts with praise." I had neither thanksgiving nor praise in my heart. I was still angry with the Lord about my situation. As I slunk in and sat down on the first available chair in the corner I felt a crushing weight of despondency on my shoulders. This was not how I had envisioned coming to church after waiting for ten long years.

In my utter misery, I even harbored the possibility of returning to Islam if it meant keeping my family together, but I wanted to let Jesus decide that for me, so I told him "Jesus, I want to go back to Islam because I want my husband and my children. If you are truly a caring God, then I want you to prove it now or I go back. So I'm asking you to bring my husband into this church."

I thought this would be very difficult for the Lord. Ilyas wouldn't even allow me to go to church; so why would he ever bother to come to church himself? Then I thought, supposing Jesus brought him ten years later, how would that prove the point? So I decided to set a time frame. "Jesus, bring him in within the next 20 minutes by my watch." That was not enough. I wanted to make it even more difficult. I said, "Bring him here within the next 20 minutes and make him sit on that chair." And I pointed out to a chair in the room.

The audacity with which I spoke to God is shocking, but please bear in mind I was extremely distraught. I really needed God's assurance that all these years of waiting on him had not been in vain. Please don't ever talk to God like this yourself. This is not a good example to emulate.

And then came the hard part, the waiting. It seemed more stressful waiting for the next few minutes to pass by than it did the past decade, but exactly within the next 20 minutes, I saw the door of the hall open and my husband walk in and sit on the very chair I had pointed out to Jesus. Did I need further proof of God's awesome goodness and love? I wanted to jump up and praise him, but worship was already over and the preaching of the Word was in progress. I observed that Ilyas was listening attentively to the sermon.

When it was time to go home, the cold war continued between us; no talking, only silence. This lasted a whole week until the next Sunday, when I began to get ready to go out again. My husband asked me, "Where are you going?" I replied, "To New Life A.G. Church." I stood, rooted to the spot in amazement, when I heard him call, "Wait for me. I am coming."

All talk of divorce had mysteriously vanished and we continued to attend church together in this awkward manner. I thought that his only reason for coming was to watch over me, but my theory was proved wrong about eight months later. One particular rainy Sunday, I was burning with a fever, so I told my husband that I wouldn't be going to church as I wasn't feeling too well. I fully expected him to remain behind with me, so you can imagine my shock when he said, "OK, you stay at home. I will go and come." I realized then that the Lord had been drawing Ilyas to himself as well, and that he hadn't been coming for my sake alone. God had touched his heart, causing him to become an avid seeker of the truth himself.

Rejoicing Together in the Lord

One year later Ilyas gave his heart to the Lord in complete surrender. The first thing he confessed to us was that he wished he had not wasted all these long years in making this decision for Christ. But I rejoiced that my ten years of praying and waiting had finally been rewarded. Praise the Lord!

Shortly after his conversion, my husband said, "Why don't we dedicate our living room to Jesus and you can begin a Bible Study in it?" I was very happy and under the guiding eye of Arlene Stubbs, our pastor's wife, we opened our house up for the study of the Scriptures. Our Bible Study attracted many ladies from far and near and the room would be packed on Wednesday evenings. We saw God work powerfully in the hearts of all those who came to hear and receive his Word. Meanwhile, even as my Senior Pastor C.E Stubbs guided me, I continued to get trained and equipped in the study of the Holy Scriptures and sat for many exams. After passing them successfully, I finally received my credentials with the Assemblies of God.

Churches in the city began to invite me to preach and teach in their congregations, and then other churches in surrounding states began to hear of me and invite me as well. In a short while I found myself traveling to different cities in India preaching and teaching the Word of God. I had finally begun walking out my destiny in the Lord.

One day I was invited to preach in a Women's Conference in the West of India. After sharing my testimony at that conference, some ladies came up to me bristling with objections and said, "We cannot fully believe your testimony until you prove it to us from the Word of God." They were referring to my spiritual experience and the blood on my thumb and they wanted it substantiated from the Scriptures.

I was a bit taken aback at being questioned in this manner. I thought for a while and replied, "OK, I think I can substantiate my spiritual experience from verse 3 in Paul's second letter to the Corinthians in chapter 12, where he writes of a man being transported to the third heaven. Now that is really high, but as for me, I went up only to the nearest cloud. So it is true that one can have an out of body experience as I did. The Scripture also records numerous other examples like John and Ezekiel and Elijah, who were also taken up in the spirit and transported to other places."

"What about the blood on your thumb?" they insisted. For

that, however, I had no immediate answer. On the train ride home, upset and unnerved, I turned to Jesus and told Him, "I will not share my testimony again until you prove to me from your Word that the blood on my thumb was a valid sign from you."

The following Wednesday I had to prepare for my Ladies' weekly Bible study, and in my time of preparation the Lord led me to read from the book of Exodus. I had read this book so many times before, but somehow this particular passage had escaped my attention. Now as the Lord led me to chapter 29, I began to read very carefully. This chapter deals with God's instructions to Moses for the consecration of the priesthood which was a very solemn and holy ceremony.

Exodus 29:1 says, The Lord told Moses, *"This is what you are to do to consecrate them* (Aaron and his sons so they may serve me as priests). *Take a young bull and two rams without defect."* Here God was speaking about the consecration of priests so they may serve him. God tells Moses further in the chapter to slaughter the bull, take its blood and put it on the horns of the altar. . . "Take one of the rams and Aaron and his sons shall lay their hands on its head, slaughter it, take the blood and sprinkle it against the altar on all sides."

Then in verse 19 of that chapter he says,

"Take the other ram, and Aaron and his sons shall lay their hands on its head. Slaughter it, take some of its blood and put it on the lobes of the right ears of Aaron and his sons, ON THE THUMBS OF THEIR RIGHT HANDS, and on the big toes of their right feet. Then sprinkle blood against the altar."

All this was meant to be done to consecrate the priests who would be serving the Lord.

I closed my Bible and wept in repentance for still doubting

him. I cried, "Lord, your ways are far above our ways. O God, You are so specific. You could have put that drop of blood on any part of my body, any part of my hand, my palms or my fingers, but you are a God who operates according to your Word, never contradicting it. You chose to put that drop of blood specifically on my right thumb to be in agreement with Scripture. You literally consecrated me to serve you as a priest before any man, organization or church could do it. How beautifully you led me step by step. First you caused conviction in my heart, and then led me to repentance and to pray for the forgiveness of my sins. Then you gave me the joy and the assurance of forgiveness through a spiritual experience. Only after that did you put the blood of consecration on my right thumb. When you put that blood I didn't even understand what it meant, but you knew what you were doing in setting me apart to be used in your service.

"You are far above gender; you did this for me, a woman. You are far above culture and creed. Who should have been consecrated? Not a woman; certainly not a Muslim woman; yet you put your mark of consecration on me even before I knew and accepted Jesus Christ as my personal Saviour. You are above every race, every religion, and every ritual. You are very great O God. Thank you."

Since then, in fulfillment of his promise and call, God has taken me to the nations to teach and tell many that Jesus is the Christ. Every time I think of his goodness and faithfulness, I am awed afresh. He said, "Go to the nations," and I am still going. He said no one will hurt you and thus far, he is still my Ebenezer. He took me, a simple, ordinary Muslim woman, one who was not allowed to set foot inside a mosque, and placed me behind many pulpits. God has done marvelous things, wonderful things. He is the same yesterday, today and forever, the Almighty One, the Holy One, and the Magnificent One.

Why has this testimony been shared? To prove the truth of God's Word which he spoke in prophecy through Joel 2:28: *"And afterward I will pour out my Spirit on all people. Your sons and daughters will prophesy, your old men will dream dreams, your young men will see visions. Even on my servants, both men and women, I will pour out my Spirit in those days."*

This prophecy included Muslim women because he was speaking of all flesh. I marvel at the sovereignty of God. He cannot be restricted in his ways in trying to reach out to the perishing. He can use anybody, just anybody, to fulfill his plans. He used a Protestant Christian woman, Madhubala Ernest, to pray for me and Neelam Edwards and Nirmala Abraham to befriend me. He used a Catholic priest, James D'Souza to share the gospel, he used a missionary couple of the Mennonite Brethren, Henry and Amanda Poetker, to disciple me over the phone for at least 7 years before my husband accepted the Lord. He used a Pentecostal American of the Assemblies of God, Ps. C.E Stubbs, to be my spiritual father and guide, and to acknowledge the gifts of God in my life well enough to recommend my being credentialed with the Assemblies of God. God is unique. He is a God of variety, picking up anyone and using anyone according to his purpose.

Why did I share this testimony? Just to let my readers know that I was not discontented with my religion. I began to believe and follow Jesus because of what he did to me and the call he laid on my life.

Why did I share this testimony? To let my readers know that before God, men and women are both of great value. He picked me up, a woman, a Muslim woman, a married Muslim woman who had never entered the precincts of a mosque, even though there was one very close to her residence. God picked me, communicated with me, convicted me, commissioned me and put me in the very house of God to serve him. I pray that the Lord who gave his life for me will continue to give me the privilege and honor of serving him, because he consecrated me for this very reason.

To God be all the glory!

2

$\mathcal{I}$n His Time

Ilyas' Testimony

I was born into a privileged family with the proverbial silver spoon in my mouth. My father was a high ranking executive and was the first Indian to be appointed as Mint Master in the Indian Government. He had completed his education in London which only an elite few could afford in those days and it had paid off. Working for the government was a much coveted appointment with many perks and much prestige. Life was cushy for me while growing up, but apart from material comforts, I was blessed to have a family that was liberal and moderate in their outlook towards life and religion.

During my father's stint in England as a student and a paying guest, he made a very favorable impression on his landlady who had been closely watching his systematic and principled lifestyle. She seemed very impressed with his cultured and polite demeanor, and one day she ingenuously remarked, "Yousuf, you are a very good Christian." My father graciously decided to accept that as a compliment.

My mother was fortunate to have had a liberal education

as well, considering the fact that she was a Muslim girl. All the teachers in her school were European and she graduated from High School with a Distinction, for which she was awarded a gold medal.

I remember my mother as being a very prayerful person. She was deeply devout and religious and would spend long hours in prayer and worship, yet she possessed a gentle wisdom in her heart which transcended any form of rigid religiosity.

As a child I often used to wonder what Allah must look like and would try and visualize him in my mind, but however much I tried to imagine him, he still seemed a mysterious, distant, esoteric figure to me. Yet, somewhere deep within me, even from a young age, there was a strong leaning towards things spiritual.

When I was about 7 years old my mother taught me how to perform the *salat* (the obligatory prayers performed 5 times a day) and how to worship Allah properly. I was taught that to pray 5 times a day was Allah's command; I could be excused from praying my *namaz* (salat) only if I was sick or traveling; those were the only good enough reasons for abstaining. Otherwise it is mandatory for all boys above 12 years of age to worship Allah *Ta'ala* (Exalted be he). I knew no other god except Allah and my heart desired to please him above everything else, even from such a young age.

Teenage Angst

My teenage years, however, were not too easy. Apart from the usual angst associated with that age, I began to develop a morbid apprehension over the fate of my sins. At an age when most youngsters are interested in living life to the full and having a good time, I was agonizing over the destiny of my soul. Would I make it to heaven or to hell—that was my constant query. There was no explicit assurance in my religion that Allah would definitely forgive all my sins or that my soul was destined for salvation; in my fear-filled mind, hell seemed a more distinct possibility for me, and plagued with these dark thoughts, I would wallow in the depths of depression, desperate to know the answers to many questions in my heart.

My mother was extremely distressed over this state of my mind. She tried to help me the best she could, but to no avail. One day when I was deep in the mire of depression she sat on my bed and said to me, "My son, I cannot bear to see you so unhappy and dismal. My prayers for you don't seem to be working either and I don't know why not. But I long to see you happy and if it means that you need to change your religion in order to overcome your depression and lead a happier life, then go ahead and do it."

I was shocked. Such advice coming from my religious Muslim mother impacted me deeply and I never forgot those words all my life. But of course, changing my religion was simply not an option for me at all. As far as I was concerned, there could be no better religion than Islam.

Marital Bliss

In due course it was time for me to get married and my mother began to make enquiries for a suitable bride for me. My future wife's cousin who was a match-maker, told my mother that she had the perfect bride for me from across the Tank Bund; the reservoir of water that separated the twin cities of Hyderabad and Secunderabad. So a meeting was set up and in a common gathering of relatives, I saw my future bride for the first time.

When they pointed her out to me, I was pleasantly surprised to see that she was quite beautiful, but throughout the evening I felt as though I was back in school again. She conducted herself as though she was teaching a classroom of students. We never spoke directly to each other but I observed her every move and watched how she carried herself. She seemed intelligent and confident of herself, quite unlike the traditionally demure brides I had been accustomed to viewing. My mother, however, decided that she was good enough to become her "bahu" or daughter in law, and so my parents approached her parents with a proposal of marriage, and an auspicious date was set for my marriage with Safia.

My cousin thought she was an excellent choice for me, but my youngest brother was a bit apprehensive. After seeing how articulate and intelligent she was, he remarked that she seemed "razor sharp." I agreed with both their opinions.

Marriage, however, turned out to be a pleasant enough experience, even though we had tremendous differences in personality and temperament. I was a practicing Muslim who prayed five times a day, fasting every year for the full 30 days and attending every religious function I could. I had a deep, abiding faith in Islam and considered no other religion anywhere as good as mine. My wife, on the other hand, didn't seem to be as devout as I was. She tended to be a bit haphazard in her prayer life compared to my mother and me; although there was no doubt that she certainly was a staunch believer. Her devotion to Allah was never in question and her love for him was very real.

Marital Discord

Besides practicing all the mandatory rituals in Islam, I would also visit all the tombs of the saints; the *dargahs* and *mazars* of holy men. I had a great love for the Prophet Muhammad's son-in-law Hazrat Ali who was our first Imam. I would make regular visits every Thursday to a hill on which it was believed that Hazrat Ali had imprinted his hand and his knee, carrying flowers and incense sticks to offer at this holy site; hoping that he would grant the many petitions I made to him.

Our marriage continued in an uneventful manner with no major hiccups as I learned to adjust to my wife's capable and swift way of doing things, while she likewise adjusted to my staid and sedate life-style. We were soon blessed with a cherished daughter and Safia continued working as a teacher in St Ann's High School, fulfilling both roles capably and efficiently.

We were only in our fourth year of marriage when the crisis hit us. It is true that I had encouraged her to attend the prayer meeting in which she had that intense spiritual experience, but I was completely unprepared for the shocking turn of events which followed. It was the last thing I would have ever expected and the remotest speck of possibility on my horizon. It was the day my wife announced that she had decided to become a Christian.

"Are you absolutely sure you know what you are doing?" I probed her. "Is this what you really want?" I had to be convinced that she was aware of the consequences and was not reacting to a spiritual euphoria that would soon evaporate. She must know that she faced rejection not only from me, but from the whole community. She would never again be able to walk anywhere with her head held high and the possibility of unfriendly retaliation from orthodox believers would always haunt her every step. But she unhesitatingly and firmly replied, "Yes." and seemed convinced that she knew what she was doing and was aware of all the possible consequences of that decision.

Then I looked within my own heart. Would I be able to live with a woman who had converted to another religion which I considered quite second-class? From my one-dimensional viewpoint, I had always considered Christian women as loose and immoral. In my opinion, they dressed indecently and lived fast lives. Would I be able to face my family and friends, knowing that they shared the same outlook as me? Could I be brave enough to support her against the expected onslaughts of our community and family?

I looked long and hard at her and our daughter and then I decided I cared too much for them both to break up my happy family. What she believed in was her personal choice and I could not change that. Moreover, the Koran did make allowances for Muslim men to marry women from the People of the book, the *Ahl-e-kitab*, so I was not violating any rules of my religion. Perhaps if I showed kindness and understanding as a good Muslim husband, she might even revert to Islam one day.

So I told her, "All right, you can follow Jesus Christ if you want, but I would prefer you to not go to church while you are under my roof. You can read your Bible at home but that is as much as I am prepared to accept at this stage."

Relatives' Reactions

The reaction from our relatives was naturally one of shocked outrage, but for some strange reason, it was quite muted compared to what we had actually anticipated. Some were of the opinion that she had gone completely out of her mind and tried to convince me to get her examined by a doctor. I observed her carefully to see if that was so, but she seemed normal enough and there seemed nothing in her behaviour to cause me alarm about her mental state. She still continued to work and look after our daughter and the home efficiently and calmly.

But there was one thing I noticed which was startlingly uncharacteristic about her now. In our four years of married life I had probably seen her praying about three or four times only; now she spent long hours praying and reading her Bible. Every opportunity she got, I found her buried in the book or deep in prayer. It brought back memories of my mother who used to spend long hours in prayer as well.

However, when my relatives saw that Safia continued to follow her new faith staunchly, they began to urge me to take control of the situation and not let it deteriorate further. Some even indirectly suggested that I should put her away. I was warned that as her husband if I didn't take her in hand, I would be the one responsible for all further negative consequences, and I was strongly encouraged to bring her back to the faith and negate whatever spiritual influence she had come under.

In the midst of this storm and turbulence, there was only one calm voice that dared to say something different. It came from a man I respected tremendously, and this learned, discerning man sent me a message through a mutual friend that I should not be worried or doubtful about what had happened to Safia. He believed that she had certainly and definitely been touched by God. I was grateful for that assurance and encouraged myself in it.

However, the rest of the family continued to seek different ways to bring her back on the right track. One of my relatives suggested that we take her to a particular *maulvi* (spiritual teacher) who was very learned in both the Bible and the Koran. He had studied the *Tauret* (Old Testament) the *Injil* (New Testament) and the Koran-e-sharif for seven years and would be the perfect person to consult and to prove to my wife the discrepancies and corruption in the Bible.

The Dialogue

So we went to visit this esteemed man of God and after some preliminary talk and introductions told him the purpose of our visit. He immediately went in and brought out a big Bible and placing it on a decorative stand, sat down. He looked so saintly in his white garb and his head gear. Then he asked my wife to tell him all that had happened and how she had suddenly come to believe in Jesus Christ. She told him everything. Then he looked at her and said seriously, "I wish to tell you, please come back to Islam. This faith has been founded by Allah and is the true faith. The Bible has been thoroughly corrupted."

Opening the Bible to Deuteronomy 18:15 he read out, The LORD your God will raise up for you a prophet like me from among your own brothers. You must listen to him; continuing from verse 17, he read,

"I will raise up for them a prophet like you from among their brothers: I will put my words in his mouth and he will tell them everything I command him. If anyone does not listen to my words that the prophet speaks in my name, I myself will call him to account."

He shut the book and turning to my wife said, "Can't you see that the prophet Moses is talking about our honorable prophet? This is in reference to him. We are to listen to him, so come back to the faith."

My wife prayed silently and then answered, "Excuse me *maulvi sahib*, (Teacher sir) but the prophet referred to here is Jesus Christ because the reference to 'your brothers' is to the Israelites and not to the Ishmaelites. This prophet was definitely Jesus who was an Israelite; not the honorable Prophet Muhammad who was an Ishmaelite, may his soul rest in peace." We were all a little shocked as to how she not only knew the answer but that she could rebut an esteemed scholar like him so boldly.

Then the *maulvi* opened to John 14:16. He said," Do you know that even Jesus Christ referred to our prophet?" and he read what Jesus said, *"And I will ask the Father and he will give you another Counselor to be with you forever—the Spirit of truth. The world cannot accept him because it neither sees him nor knows him. But you know him for he lives with you and will be in you."* He then proceeded to explain that the Comforter who Jesus was referring to was none other than our honorable prophet because the prophet's other name Ahmed is very close in meaning to the word Comforter. "Even Jesus Christ refers to our prophet in this verse," he stated.

All of us who were listening intently, thought, now she's cornered. Now she'll have to come back. I could see my wife praying silently again and then she replied, "Excuse me *maulvi sahib,* but the Comforter referred to here by Jesus Christ cannot be the prophet, because he said that the world cannot see him as he is a spirit, but the world could definitely see our prophet, and this verse also refers to the fact that the Comforter will live with us and be in us forever.

"With all due respect," she continued, "we cannot see our prophet because he is dead and his grave in Medina is visited by millions of followers, so he is not the one who will live with us forever. Nor is he the one who will live in us because God will raise him along with the rest of mankind. This is surely the Holy Spirit, which those who believe in Christ will receive as a gift from God and as a power to help us live in this sinful world."

The *maulvi* made one last attempt, "Do you know something? Jesus Christ never died on the cross."

"So who was that on the cross then, *maulvi sahib?*" my wife asked.

He replied, "Allah made someone else to look like Jesus Christ and the people caught him and they crucified him instead."

"Who was the person who was made to look like Jesus?" she asked.

The *maulvi* thought for some time and then said, "It was Judas Iscariot."

There was a pause followed by a question from my wife. "Why do you think it was Judas Iscariot?

My head began reeling from this volleying back and forth of questions and answers, and I could see that the esteemed scholar was beginning to get hot under the collar at all this arrogant questioning by a woman.

He replied, "It was Judas Iscariot because had it been Jesus Christ, he would never have said, "My God, my God why have you forsaken me? Allah never forsakes his prophets."

My wife thought for some time, all the while praying silently, and then she said, "Excuse me *maulvi sahib*. I think it was definitely Jesus Christ who was crucified, because had it been Judas he would never have said, "Father, forgive them for they know not what the do. Such words can come only from Jesus Christ, not his betrayer."

There was a moment of stunned silence after this reply; then the *maulvi* got up, picked up his book, turned on his heels and without another word went back inside. We had thought that by taking her to this wise man, she would recant and return to the faith with deep repentance. But just the opposite had happened. She had an answer for everything and seemed more established now than before.

"I told you we shouldn't have brought her here. She is too sharp," I told my relatives. They were all the more concerned about me now. With such a bold wife who could rebut even an esteemed scholar, what hope did I have left? So they never missed an opportunity to extol the virtues of Islam as the best religion in the world and to remind me that since I was a pillar of the community I must uphold it all the more faithfully and practice it more devoutly.

Healing of Migraine

Life continued to drag on with neither of us really enjoying any true spiritual harmony, though physically we lived a normal family life. God blessed us with a wonderful son and my wife continued to stand firm and unwavering in her faith. She had still not gone inside any church to worship in deference to my wishes. She only continued to read the Bible diligently and pray a lot. I prided myself on being a tolerant and understanding husband, but even though I could see an incredible transformation in my wife which left a profound impression on me, I was still unwilling to consider that she could ever be right in her religious convictions.

One of the fall outs from my early years of depression were my constant and blindingly severe headaches. I would suffer with migraine for days and be quite incapacitated each time I had an attack. One day my wife returned from her school and told me that there was going to be a healing meeting in one of the churches in our vicinity, and asked if I wanted to be prayed over for my headaches. I thought it couldn't do me any harm, so I agreed to go.

After the speaker delivered his message, which I listened to quite distractedly, he asked who all would like healing prayer for any ailments they were suffering from. Hands shot up all across the crowded compound. Emboldened by so many people asking for prayer, I too raised my hand. The Mother Superior of the Convent, Sister Annetta, noticed me standing there with a raised hand and along with three others approached me and gently asked me what my need was. I told her, "I get severe headaches. I want healing."

The group then laid their hands on me and prayed for healing in Jesus' name. After their prayer, Sister Annetta asked me, "Do you believe in Jesus Christ?"

I answered, "Yes, of course I believe in him. I believe that he was one of the greatest prophets that God sent."

But she answered me, "No no, you must also believe in him as the Son of God."

That was too hard for me to accept, it was blasphemy to my ears. How could I commit *shirk* (sin of idolatry) by worshiping any god other than Allah? I just turned away and came back home.

But one thing was undeniable. This Prophet *Isa* (Jesus) could certainly heal. I never ever suffered from those headaches again and I was extremely grateful for that. I acknowledged to myself that there certainly was undeniable power in the name of Jesus Christ.

Bank Transfer

By profession I was a banker and I worked as a Branch Manager in the State Bank of India. One day I received the news that I was to be transferred to a village branch in Cherial district in the State of Andhra Pradesh. I had lived and worked all my life in the city and could not imagine being transferred to a village branch. I especially dreaded going to that particular place as I had heard that it was infested with poisonous snakes and frogs. I was very disappointed and tried my best to get out of it, so I appealed to all my superiors but with no success. There was no way I could get out of this transfer; I would have to manage my Bank's branch in the village and that was that.

One of my relatives told me that he knew of a particular maulvi who possessed immense spiritual powers and he suggested that I go to him for prayer to stop the transfer. So I met the man and told him my problem. He first presented me with a long list of non-refundable items that I would need to supply him with—2 kg of fish, 2 kg of chicken, 10 kg of rice and 5 kg of pulses—all these before he would even begin to pray for me. I was desperate enough to willingly give him anything to stop the transfer. After receiving all his grocery requirements, he then proceeded to chant some prayers in order to block the transfer. I then returned home, lighter in the pocket, but happy and relieved that I would not have to leave my familiar surroundings.

To my utter shock, the transfer orders were still on my table when I returned to work the next day. Nothing had changed in the office, not even after 2 months of waiting. So I went back to the maulvi and told him that his prayers had achieved nothing. He simply shrugged his shoulders and told me, "Look, I did the best I could and you've tried everything as well. I suggest you now go and cling to the feet of the 8th Imam of the Shia Muslims and call on his name by faith, and he will see to it that your transfer will not come about."

Quite disillusioned, I turned to go home when a strange notion suddenly floated into my mind. "Why should I cling to the feet of a dead man? No denying that he was a holy man, a saint, but he was still dead. So what good could the dead do for the living?"

I began to wrestle silently with this unexpected chain of thought. The better part of my life had been spent seeking favors from dead men and burning incense at their tombs without these thoughts ever entering my mind; now all of a sudden I was consumed with this paradoxical problem.

Then quite as suddenly, the logical answer seemed to present itself as well. "Wouldn't it be far better to cling to the feet of a living prophet like Jesus Christ? The Koran states that Jesus is alive and will be returning at the end of the age. Wouldn't he be a more logical choice for help?" I mulled over this matter and in the end decided against going to any dead saint's shrine. But I didn't bother to ask Jesus Christ for help either. I was still too afraid to connect with anything Christian.

To reach Cherial district I had to take three buses and travel over rough terrain and dusty roads to reach my destination. It was an undeveloped village and had none of the amenities that I was accustomed to. I struggled to settle in to my new surroundings and longed for the old and familiar. I missed my family tremendously as well.

A Committed Foreigner

One weekend I was at the Cherial district bus terminal waiting to catch a bus to work when I noticed a petite, middle-aged American lady pass near me. She seemed very much at home in these surroundings and my curiosity was aroused. What was a person like her doing in this forsaken place so far removed from the comforts and conveniences of her own country?

A few days later, I saw her again as I was crossing the street, and this time I greeted her politely "Good morning."

She responded amiably. "Good morning" and we struck up a conversation.

"I am Beulah White from New York," she introduced herself, "and I have been living here for the past 17 years."

I was quite astounded and asked her what had kept her so many years here. She replied that she was serving as the Principal of a Bible School that had been established there and loved the place and work immensely. It was an eye-opener to me and I was convicted by the fact that a foreigner could have such commitment and joy in living and serving the people here. It served as a stark contrast to my own attitude.

Invitation to a Prayer Meeting

We used to meet off and on, the streets, the market or the bus stop, and we would always exchange pleasantries with each other. One day she invited me to a prayer meeting at the Bible School. Not being conversant with the Telugu language, I declined at first, then later changed my mind and decided to accept her invitation. I arrived a bit early so Ms Beulah took me inside to introduce me to the Pastor who would be leading the service. As she drew back the curtain of the room he was in, we stopped short as we saw that he was already deep in prayer. Completely oblivious to our presence, he was crying his heart out to God, pleading for his presence and blessing upon the meeting. The sight of that intimate communion with God impacted me deeply. This humble man was on his knees consecrating himself so ardently for just a simple prayer meeting of uneducated, illiterate villagers. I was impressed. We backed off silently and quickly, hesitant to interrupt such glorious fellowship and I could not help comparing him to our own *mullahs* in whom worship seemed devout but almost mechanical and emotionless. This man seemed to be really communicating with a Living God.

Needless to say, even though I could not understand a word that was spoken in the meeting that followed, I felt a very definite presence of something unique in the atmosphere, something I had never felt before. The meeting was charged with passion and zeal and I saw simple village folk transformed into a people gripped by a spirit of intense prayer.

One day Ms Beulah informed me that she was going to the big city for some purchases so I told her that she must meet my wife. They met for lunch and she returned to the village with glowing reports of the wonderful time she'd had with my sweet and pretty wife.

Home Again

Life continued in this uneventful manner for a couple of years more and after serving in various villages, I was finally transferred back to my hometown. It was wonderful to be home again, and on my return I embraced my religious activities with even greater fervor. I would rise up very early in the morning, bathe and cleanse myself ritually, and then visit a particular mosque 12 km away for my morning prayers. People would admire my zeal and commend me for the fact that I was so disciplined and diligent in my worship. It made me feel good to receive their praise.

One day at work, my uncle dropped by to transact some business in the bank and requested me to step out for a moment as he wanted to talk to me in private.

He told me, "When I was in Dublin studying for my Masters Degree, I had a Roman Catholic priest as one of my professors and he liked me so much and was so impressed with me, that he wanted to convert me to his religion. I told him it was absurd for a Muslim to ever think of becoming a Christian, because being a Muslim is like being a College Graduate (since Islam superseded and followed almost 600 years after Christianity), whereas a Christian is like being a High School Graduate. Why would a College Graduate want to demote himself to become a High School Graduate?"

Having said this, he laughed at his own brilliant rhetoric and went on his way, but I understood the deeper implication that was meant for my ears only; the warning to remain a Muslim, no matter what. There was no doubt that we were the more enlightened and superior religion. I truly believed that Islam superseded and cancelled out all previous scriptures that were not in alignment with God's final revelation, the glorious Koran.

The Search Begins

When I returned home that evening however, I began pondering over what my uncle had told me and suddenly a thought began to form in my mind, "How is it that I could have graduated from college without first studying for my High School examination? Shouldn't I have first known the High School curriculum before studying for the college syllabus?"

That same night, very quietly, I picked up my wife's Bible and began to read the High School syllabus. I found myself fascinated by the simple truths that began to unravel before my eyes and was riveted by facts I had been completely unaware of. The books of

Psalms and Proverbs fascinated me with their heartfelt, honest worship and wisdom, and my interest and appreciation began to grow everyday as I found myself wanting to know more and understand more.

But in spite of my growing openness towards the Bible, the tension between my wife and I continued to build up because our spirits were still so opposite. I was beginning to feel I could not take this dichotomous life any longer and I was getting concerned for my children. They were receiving no religious education from either of us, and I could see that they were getting confused and stretched between both our religions. We were not making a good or positive impact on their lives at all. One day I found myself exploding over some trivial matter at home and then I blurted out to Safia that I wanted to divorce her. There was a stunned silence after I dropped that bombshell; then she just quietly turned and walked away.

New Life

The next day, Sunday, I found her all dressed up and ready to go out. I asked her, "Where are you going?" and she answered, "To New Life Assembly of God church." There was no way I could stop her now since I had already told her that we were going to separate, so I let her go, but after a while I felt this strange and powerfully compelling desire within me to go after her. I found the Conference Room where the church met and I walked in and sat on an empty chair to observe what was happening there.

As I entered the hall, I was caught up in the flow of the service and the message that was being preached from the pulpit attracted my interest. I paid complete attention every time the Pastor preached about God, but every time he spoke about the Son of God, it would make me so uneasy I would cringe and ignore what he was saying. Yet there was something very special in the atmosphere of that church that kept drawing me back week after week. I didn't know then that it was the manifest presence of God.

What I really enjoyed listening to were the children's sermons that the Pastor's wife, Arlene Stubbs gave every Sunday. She told the Bible stories in such an interesting and enjoyable way that I would learn and understand more from her simple stories than from the sometimes difficult and hard to understand (though theologically sound) sermons that the Senior Pastor preached.

One Sunday, after service, I decided to approach the Pastor's wife and ask her a question. "Why do the Christians make the sign of the cross?" I asked. "They commit every kind of sin under the sun and then at the end of the day, all they do is make the sign of the cross and then forget all about their sins. What sense does that make and how does it help?"

She gave me a biblical answer in a very kind manner. "Ilyas, it's not the way you think," she explained gently. "If a person sins and then simply makes the sign of the cross without true repentance in his heart, and goes back to his sinful ways the next day, his sins are definitely not going to be forgiven. God is very serious about our sins and very serious about our repentance. After all he paid a heavy price for us to receive this free gift of forgiveness and salvation. If we abuse this gift he will judge us but if we receive it with thanks, he will forgive and receive us in heaven."

She then proceeded to explain that we have to make a complete confession of our sins and repent sincerely in our hearts to God, to acknowledge Jesus as Savior and Lord and ask him to forgive us our sins. When we do that, God then forgives all the sins that have separated us from him, and Jesus comes in the form of the Holy Spirit to live in our hearts. This Holy Spirit then guides us in the way of truth and leads us away from sin.

Suddenly, everything seemed to make sense! It was as though the penny just slipped into the correct slot finally and everything became crystal clear. All these past years, even when I had tried so hard to do penance for my sins, somehow deep down I had instinctively known that it was impossible to reach an unreachable God through my own efforts. That deep-seated doubt was what had caused me such depression in my younger years. But now it was as though a light had suddenly shone brightly dispelling all my doubts and fears. I realized that God had made provision for me to approach him by opening the way to himself through the sacrifice of Jesus, and all I had to do was simply believe that he had taken my place and my punishment, and I would be set free!

As that revelation entered my heart, I simply and quietly bowed my head, confessed my sins, accepted Jesus and became his disciple. There were no great fireworks and no powerful earthquakes that accompanied my conversion. I just simply and earnestly accepted the revealed truth and in obedience responded to it, by making Jesus Christ the Lord of my life; and ever since that day 18 years ago, I have felt the direction and leading of the Holy Spirit at all times.

As you can expect, there was great rejoicing between Safia and me, and with my heart overflowing, I confessed to her that I had certainly wasted ten whole years of my life by not receiving this wonderful salvation and assurance earlier. When my relatives and friends heard this news, they reacted with a sense of fatalism. So Safia had won in the end, was their attitude. She had succeeded in converting me after all. Only I knew this was not true. She could never have done this. It was Christ and not my wife who was responsible for this conversion.

I set about zealously in my new found faith as I continued discovering new and exciting truths and testifying about them with boldness. It was not appreciated by my relatives, but God blessed me with favor and honor in my work place and elsewhere, as I shared my faith with all I came in contact with.

Fruit of Persistent Prayer

Some months after I accepted the Lord, I met Beulah White waiting at the bus stop, reading a book. She was happy to see me when I greeted her, but told me she was sad because her time in India had come to an end, and she would be returning home for good after completing her mission.

"Beulah, I have accepted the Lord Jesus as my Savior. I am now born again," I announced to her.

Her blue eyes filled with joyful tears and she gave grateful thanks to God for giving her the privilege of being a part of that process. It was only then that I discovered that she had been praying for my salvation since the first time she had met me, and had even put my name down on a prayer list from which people all over the world had been praying for me for so many years.

I am living proof of the wonder-working power of prayer. My heart's deep longing and desire is that my people, my friends, my relatives and all who read this book will also experience what I did that day when I accepted the Lord Jesus Christ as the Savior of my soul; that is the assurance of my sins being fully forgiven and hope for eternal life.

Though it took me so many years to recognize the grace of God following me wherever I went, I pray that when you are accosted with that same grace, whether through a word of testimony or through an inward conviction in your spirit, you would not harden your heart as I did, but that you would hasten to accept so great a salvation- a free gift from the Savior himself.

Jesus assures us in John 5:24, *"I tell you the truth, whoever hears my word and believes him who sent me has eternal life and will not be condemned; he has crossed over from death to life."* If I had only known this when I was wrestling with the agony of not knowing the fate of my soul, I would have been spared years of uncertainty and anguish. May the Lord bless you and shine the light of his grace in your hearts as well.

3

The Only Way
Vizarath's Testimony

My entry into this world was extremely traumatic. I was wedged in a breech position in my mother's womb and she travailed in labor for many hours before giving up exhausted. Although the doctor succeeded in delivering me, I was given up for dead as there were no visible indications of life in my tiny frail body. All attention was focussed on saving my mother instead. It was only when a nurse saw me move ever so slightly and heard a squeak from my direction that they realized I was still alive. It was by God's grace alone that I survived the ordeal of my birth on October 26, 1953.

My unpromising arrival into this world set the tone for my physical and emotional development. I was very weak and frail as a child, succumbing to every infection that visited my school or family, and suffering from myriad allergies. My whole body would often break out in angry red boils which would itch terribly and leave devastating scars on my skin. I looked and felt so horrible that melancholia was a constant companion of mine. My mother never fully recovered her strength and vitality after my birth as well, and that laid a greater burden of guilt on my young shoulders.

Growing Years

My growing years were thus marked with much anguish and despair. Frequent medical leave from school would disrupt my academic progress to such an extent that my results suffered drastically. I would be the only child to come home with a "Fail" marked in my report card, while my siblings and cousins would come bouncing back with top marks in theirs. They would run to my proud father who would shower them with compliments, but I would run straight to my mother, bury my head in the folds of her sari, and weep dejectedly. "Why am I so stupid? Why is Allah punishing only me this way? Why can't I do well like everyone else?"

She would caress me and say, "Never mind my *jaan* (my life), it's not your fault. You have other talents and we are all proud of you." But that hardly convinced or comforted me. What other talent did I really have? Nothing that could ever win a look of approval from my father. He seemed to have given up all hope in me and the only expression I ever saw in his eyes was disappointment. That was why I would go only to my mother to sign all my miserable report cards from school, and soon my illiterate mother became an expert in signing her name efficiently.

And though she loved me unconditionally, I was still constantly plagued with misery and despondency and this inevitably turned me into an introvert with no self-confidence. All my other brothers and sisters did extremely well for themselves, but my lack of self-worth kept me in the shadow of their success.

One day when I was about ten years old, my mother took me to visit her cousin in the old city of Hyderabad. After ruffling my hair and inquiring as to how I was, he suddenly asked me, "Vizarath, do you know what your name means?"

"No I. don't," I replied. "I have never thought about the meaning of my name."

He then proceeded to enlighten me. "Your name is derived from *Vazeer-e-azam* which means Prime Minister," he said, "and since you have such an auspicious name, I predict that one day you will definitely become the Prime Minister of India. Remember me when you do and give me an important position in your cabinet, OK?" He winked and smiled at me, then gave me a sweet candy and sent me off to play.

That ego-boosting prediction captured my boyish imagination instantly, and I pictured myself sitting on a throne, surveying my entire domain. In my excitement I got all pumped up with visions of grandeur and authority, and I basked in that fantasy for a long while. How unaware I was that God certainly had plans for me to be a minister, but not of the type that I was thinking!

My sluggish academic progress in school mirrored my religious and spiritual education at home. My mother had hired an *ustad* who would come home thrice-weekly to teach us Arabic, but I just could not cope with this extra learning, and would simply not go for the lessons. It was too much for me. Arabic is a difficult enough language to learn, and I found it doubly so. I remember when my sister Safia *Apa* (elder sister) first read the Koran by herself from cover to cover, the whole family was so proud of her achievement, but I could never hope to accomplish something like that. It was impossible. So I resorted to the religion of the common man; the practices of the simple, illiterate folk who could never dream of being educated in high Islamic theology. I turned to Folk Islam with intense religious fervor.

Religious Roots

My mother was a strong influence on me as she was an ardent believer in visiting shrines and burning incense to ask for favors at the *mazars* (tombs) of dead saints. We would climb a high hill named after Hazrat Ali, our first and most revered *Imam*, because it was believed that if we visited this hill and petitioned Hazrat Ali with our needs, they would definitely be answered.

I loved accompanying my mother on these pilgrimages and would always feel spiritually charged with a force I could not explain when I worshiped at these shrines. One of the main reasons we visited so many *moulanas* (holy men) was because of my weak constitution, and our foremost petition was always for the improvement of my health. The *maulvis* would give me many talismans to wear around my neck to ward off the evil eye and I would religiously and faithfully wear them. But even though they weighed my scrawny neck down so much, they never ever seemed to work effectively, and my health didn't seem to improve one bit.

I was not very regular in doing my *namaz* (5 times daily prayers), but I would faithfully recite selective *suras* (verses) from the Koran that were supposed to keep me safe from accidents, harm and danger. Spiritual discipline wasn't one of my strong points and keeping the Ramadan fast was more of a competition with my cousins than an empowering act of faith. I participated in just enough ritual to acquire the approval of man, and the favor of Allah, but I was never what one would call a devout Muslim.

I finally lost all interest in spiritual things when I became a young man, and got enamored with the world instead. Watching movies and listening to music became my favorite past time. As my religious life deteriorated even further, I practiced only the least of what was expected of me, just to keep my mother happy.

But the root of folk Islam was deeply imbued within me. One of the rituals that I enjoyed most during the festival of Muharram was slashing my chest and back to pay my respect to Imam Hussein. People said that if you shed your blood for his sake, it was a sure ticket to heaven, so I would zealously mutilate my body for all the three martyrs, Imam Ali, Imam Hasan and Imam Hussein to increase my chances of making it to paradise. I would also clothe myself in full black for the first 12 days of Muharram and join in the singing of dirges in their remembrance.

This self-flagellation and bleeding transported me to great heights of ecstasy and I experienced Allah's approval in a very tangible way. Another rite I faithfully followed was visiting the graveyard to burn incense and to pray for the souls of the dead.

All this religious activity notwithstanding, neither my health nor my academic grades actually flourished. My results in college were so low; it took me three attempts just to graduate. My father, aware of my limited intellectual capabilities, put me to work in his printing press after I finally managed to get a degree from the most mediocre college in the city. I was given hands-on training and after four years of diligent assistance, my father was confident that I was capable of managing the printing press on my own.

My Bride and Sons

Now that I was financially stable, it was time to get married. My parents were quite aged by then and were not keeping very good health, so the responsibility of finding me a bride fell on my older sister Safia Apa. Though she had converted to Christianity two years ago, I still respected her opinion and trusted her choice of a life partner for me. She searched high and low in all the Muslim localities for a suitable bride, and when she found one that she liked very much, she sent for my approval.

The moment I saw the girl, my heart was captured. Even

her name Lateefunissa was as sweet as she looked. She was extremely petite and seemed very gentle, which was an important requirement for my sensitive soul. Her high forehead, sharp features, long flowing hair and demure manner were perfect for me. We celebrated our wedding on October 6, 1980 with much rejoicing and merriment.

In the course of time our union was blessed with two sons. But our joy was soon short-lived as both our sons turned out to be as sickly as I had been. Both suffered from the curse of asthma and would experience such debilitating attacks that we would have to rush them to hospital for oxygen every couple of weeks. My sister was able to hear my older boy wheezing desperately for air all the way in her adjoining home. It was very distressing to see my sons suffer in this way, especially when they were young and helpless.

We went to every doctor and every hospital in the city, and experimented with every alternative treatment, including Homeopathy and Ayurveda. We also visited countless *dargahs* and religious places with the hope that they would get supernaturally healed, but our sons continued to struggle with this ailment and we soon became discouraged and disheartened that they would ever live normal, healthy lives. My wife also became weaker due to all this stress and the future began to look very bleak for all of us. Even after ten years life continued to be without much hope.

On the other hand, my sister Safia *Apa* and her husband Ilyas who had converted to Christianity a while ago were flourishing, always brimming over with joy and contentment, and that annoyed me immensely. Once or twice I tried to provoke my sister into some sort of confrontation but she simply looked at me calmly and said, "The Bible tells me not to argue, so I will not argue with you, but I will only ask you one thing. My Bible tells me that Jesus loves me. Does your Koran say that your prophet loves you?" I didn't have a suitable answer to that question and that infuriated me even more.

I just could not tolerate the sight of both my sister and brother-in-law following the same apostate faith right in front of me. Ilyas Bhai (brother) tried to speak to me about Jesus Christ sometimes, but I would turn a deaf ear and walk away from him. One day I asked him, "You have been in Islam for so long and you know all about our religious leaders. How can you now turn your back on them? Don't they mean anything to you at all?"

He responded, "None of our religious leaders ever said, "I am the Way, the Truth and the Life." Only Jesus did. Which choice makes better sense to you?"

I had no answer to that and I was angry with myself for not being able to shake the faith of my sister and her husband.

Asthma Healed

In August 1990, my sister invited a visiting evangelist who had a gift of healing to her house for lunch. Before he arrived, she came to me and said, "Vizarath, there is a man of God with a gift of healing who is coming to my house for a meal. Why don't you ask him to pray for your sons and if God wills, he will heal them? After all, what do you have to lose?"

I thought about it and then discussed it with my wife. It was true, what did we have to lose? Nothing else had worked so far, and if this man's prayer did work, then at least my children would not have to suffer so much. We were very desperate to see them healed quickly; we just couldn't bear to see them suffering so much.

So I asked my wife, "Shall I take the children and have them prayed over?" She thought about it for a while, then said, "Take them and go but don't close your eyes even for a minute when he's praying, otherwise he might mesmerize you and the children and convert you to Christianity as well. Please be alert at all times." So, armed with this word of caution, I took my sons to my sister's house. My wife refused to accompany me.

This man of God seemed very kind and compassionate, and when I told him about the asthma, he said, "Don't worry, I will pray for your children and God willing, they will get well." He made us repeat some sort of prayer after him and after we repeated it, he laid his hands on my sons' chests and said, "In Jesus' name, I rebuke the spirit of asthma and command it to come out!"

Suddenly I began to shake and tremble from the crown of my head to the soles of my feet. I looked quickly towards my sons and saw that they were shaking as well and that their eyes had filled with tears. I looked around to see if any of the other Christian guests were having the same reaction as us, but none of them was. They were just standing around praying silently. I immediately recognized it as some sort of spiritual power encounter, but I wondered what exactly was happening. Then, as suddenly as we started, we stopped, and after thanking the evangelist for his prayer, we returned home.

My wife wanted to know what had happened there, but I didn't give her all the details as I knew it would upset her. However, I waited and watched to see the effect of that prayer. Usually our son would get an attack every two weeks and we would need to rush him to the doctor, but from that moment on they never had another bout of asthma in their lives. Never again did we ever have to take them to any doctor for that dreadful disease. They were completely and utterly healed and I was amazed. For years we had tried everything, and had spent so much money on doctors and dargahs, but now this one simple prayer in the name of Jesus had cured them completely. And it had been for free as well! I pondered on all this for a while but then, like all of selfish humanity, I just accepted the gift and ignored the Giver.

Around the same time as my sons' health woes, I began having problems with my business. The printing press had been running smoothly and successfully for about five years, but I started losing my grip on it because of my preoccupation with all the problems at home. Times had changed and competition had got keener, with machines becoming more modern and efficient. My small and antiquated printing machines didn't stand a chance with such competition and soon my business began going into fiscal loss. I had to borrow money just to survive and with the interest piling up I soon found myself in deep debt.

We were in dire financial straits and my sense of inadequacy began to weigh heavily on me again. I felt as though I had come full circle, a failure in school, a failure in college and now a failure in business as well.

Communal Threat

In December of that year, communal riots broke out in Hyderabad and there was an uprising of religious insurrection and bloodshed. I feared the worst and expected the Hindus to target me and my printing press as we were situated in a predominantly Hindu neighborhood with most of my workers being Muslim. My grim fears were justified one morning when I answered the telephone and an ominous voice threatened me, "If you don't close down your press within two hours, we will come and shoot you and your workers."

I panicked. My Muslim friend, who had been drinking tea with me when the call came, gave me some sound advice. "Don't whisper a word of this to any of your workers because they will all get scared and run away home. You just go home quietly by yourself and come back after two hours to see if they have carried out their threat or not." It didn't strike me then that this was a cowardly way out but I took his advice and rushed back home. My wife was surprised to see me home so early and asked what had happened at work.

"I received a threatening telephone call," I told her, "they want to close down the printing press." She too got scared and both of us felt extremely insecure. Then I thought of my sister Safia Apa and decided to tell her what had occurred and ask for her advice.

She listened to me quietly and then advised me, "Just be calm. Don't panic. If you want, I can pray for you, but I will pray in Jesus' name."

I was so fearful at that point in time I would have accepted prayer in anyone's name, so I agreed to her request. She interceded for us with great faith and then told me to go back to my press and not to worry. Nothing bad was going to happen to my printing press or me, she reassured me confidently, because she had surrendered the entire situation into Jesus' hands.

With those comforting words echoing in my heart I returned to my shop after the two hours deadline was up, and sure enough, nothing had been touched and no one had been shot. We were all safe for the time being, but who knew for how long? I couldn't stop looking over my shoulder every minute of the day and my fear and insecurity kept increasing.

My wife decided she had a solution to this problem. She felt that we needed to become more religious and fervent in our faith. Perhaps if we diligently said our namaz and recited more suras from the Koran every day, Allah would be gracious and keep us safe. We began to pray zealously and seek him with all our hearts, sometimes worshiping Allah till the early hours of the morning, continuously reciting all his 99 beautiful names on the rosary with great veneration.

Our piety increased a hundredfold, yet deep down in my heart there was a vacuum, an emptiness I couldn't explain. I became disenchanted with all the contradictions I saw around me and questions began forming in my soul.

"Why was there so much hatred and misery in the world— why so much bloodshed in the name of religion? If all religions are good and supposed to lead us to God, then why was there such disharmony in the world? In India, the Hindus and the Muslims fought with each other because their religions were completely diametric, but in Pakistan, the *Sunni* and the *Shia* sects of the same religion killed each other as well. If people were not fighting because of religious differences, then they were slaughtering each other on the basis of race. The Germans wanted only the Germans to remain in their country, and in South Africa, the whites were hostile to the blacks. Why was this so? Who had the answers to all these questions and where would I find it? If God was looking at all of this, what was he doing about it?"

The Search for the Way

Thus began my serious quest for the truth in the month of December, 1990. While neighbors lived in fear of each other, I began to seek for the meaning and purpose of life by reading many spiritual books and enquiring from people of all walks of life.

One day I asked my Muslim friend, "The Koran says that *Isa* is coming at the end of the world, then why don't we worship *Isa* since he is alive?"

My friend immediately retorted, "Don't go into all these details because you know that Paul has corrupted the Bible."

I was surprised at his answer. I had asked him a simple

question about *Isa* from the Koran, and he warned me against a corrupted Bible. They were two irrelevant things and didn't make sense to me but I kept it at the back of my mind and continued with my search.

Exactly a year later, I was still in the dark and my quest had yielded no results; only more questions. I had found no satisfactory answers, and no book or person had succeeded in revealing the truth to me. I was very disheartened as my life's situation continued to be the same. That was when my friend and neighbor came to me and told me, "Vizarath, you have tried so many things and I can see that you are seriously searching. So I ask you, why don't you try Jesus? Why don't you ask him to help you?"

But I wasn't as yet ready to do that, and since no man could give me an answer, I decided to put the question to Allah himself and see what he said. Perhaps, in his mercy, he would enlighten me. So on December 6, 1991, after reading my morning *Namaz*, I looked up to heaven and very simply and earnestly I asked Allah, in my own mother tongue Urdu, to please show me the way.

I said, "Allah, all these years I have been saying my *namaz* and reciting my *suras* in Arabic, in a language I do not understand. But today, for the first time in my life, I am asking you in my own language to please answer me one question. The Hindus, the Muslims, the Christians all say that their way is the right way, but I am a simple man who cannot understand all these spiritual things, so I am asking you Allah, please tell me who is right and who is wrong. Please show me the right way. If Hinduism is the right way, I will become a Hindu, if Christianity is right, I will become a Christian, if Islam is correct, then I am already a Muslim. But please Allah, I need you to specifically tell me which is the right way and whatever you show me, I will accept."

As I prayed this simple request, a stillness came over my

heart and I knew that God was somehow going to answer this sincere appeal.

The next day I had to go to the pharmacy to buy some cough medicine for my children, and as I waited for the shopkeeper to bring it out, I casually turned around to watch the noisy traffic on the busy main road. Suddenly my attention was directed to a scooter parked on the footpath and as I looked at it closely, I saw a sticker on it which read, THE LORD JESUS CHRIST IS THE ONLY WAY TO HEAVEN.

As the impact of those words struck me and I absorbed their significance, my whole body suddenly turned hot and strong currents like electricity began sparking from the top of my head down to my feet. My heart began to race very fast and I felt like the ground was going to cave in right there and then. It hit me right in the pit of my stomach. Here was my answer from Allah!

And I heard a small voice within me saying, "What did you ask, which is the right way? Is it Hinduism? No, it is not. Is it Islam? No, it is not. Is it Christianity? Not at all! It is only the Lord Jesus Christ who is The Way."

This revelation bowled me over completely. God seemed to be telling me that no religion was the right way. The right way was only in following the Person of the Lord Jesus Christ. Not a religion, but a person! Not a religion, but a person! As I digested and absorbed this radical concept, the trembling ceased in my body and I was back to normal. Yet, even though I had received such a clear and dramatic answer from God, I still waited, unsure of what I should do next.

Two days later at work I noticed my printing press was in a very messy and untidy state with papers strewn all over the floor. So I decided to stop all the machines and begin cleaning up the place. My employee tried to dissuade me from this course of action as he felt we would incur a big loss if we shut everything down. He reminded me that it would take two hours to get the machines rolling again, but I was adamant and overruled his advice and so we set about tidying up.

Suddenly, my wife's brother who was assisting me put an envelope in my hand. I asked him what it was and he replied, "Your sister had given these papers for binding a long time ago, but we forgot to do it." As I took out the papers my eyes fell on some words written on the top page, "Jesus said if you ask anything in his name, you will receive it. . . " I turned some more pages at random and read, "I will throw away your sins in the sea of forgetfulness and never fish them out again. . ."

As I read these words on her notes, I began to experience the same sensations in my body that I had the previous day in the medical store. My entire focus now became riveted completely on Jesus Christ and the message that he was trying to send to me.

Acceptance of the Way

As I pondered at length over the last two days' events in my mind, I then quietly, and without any one's prompting but God's, went to my table, bowed my head and simply believed and trusted in the Lord Jesus Christ. I trusted in his power and authority to forgive my sins and believed that he was the way to heaven. In my mind I still considered him as a Prophet of very high ranking because I had seen his effectiveness in answering prayers before. You must remember that I was a Muslim who had never read the Bible and had no idea that Jesus claimed to be God who could forgive my sin. But that day, with a simple childlike faith that I could never have mustered on my own; it had to be a gift from God; I just simply believed in Jesus Christ as my Savior.

There was an instantaneous reaction from my body to this decision. All of a sudden I felt something intangible, yet forceful, swoosh up from my stomach all the way to my neck and begin choking me for a few seconds. As I clutched my neck in fear, this force, finding no room for escape from the top, went downwards and then with a big whoosh came right out from the middle of my stomach. I felt as though I had been set free of something spiritually unclean, and as a strange peace settled in my soul, a fresh bubbling of joy began to emerge and overflow from my spirit.

Then I heard a voice speaking to my heart, "Go and confess your faith now." I got onto my scooter and raced back home. I wanted to share it with somebody who would understand, so I rushed straight to my sister who was ironing clothes, and hugged her while crying with joy, "I have accepted the Lord Jesus Christ, I have accepted the Lord Jesus Christ, and I feel something bubbling up from within me. I feel so much joy, I cannot explain it."

She was stunned but thrilled as she wept tears of gratitude. Holding me tightly she said, "I have been praying for your salvation these past fourteen years and God has finally answered my prayers. Praise the Lord!"

It seemed so foolish to me then that I had wasted one whole year struggling to find out the truth from men and from books, when all I should have done was to ask God directly. How graciously he had answered me and revealed to me that Jesus Christ was the Way and the Truth.

But confessing my new-found faith was easier said than done when it came to my wife. I was very fearful of her reaction. What if she decided to ask me for a divorce and take my sons away from me? That was a horrible prospect and I decided to be a secret believer for as long as I could. I met a young pastor who began to mentor and disciple me and I would go secretly to his house every morning to read the Bible and to learn about truth. But that was a foolish plan.

When I stopped saying my *namaz* and reciting *suras* from the

Koran, my wife obviously noticed it and questioned me. "Why have you stopped saying your *namaz*? I have been watching you. You have neither been praying nor reciting the *suras* from our holy book."

I evaded answering her truthfully and just assured her that I would do it later. But in a short while she noticed that I still wasn't conducting all my rituals and began insisting that I do so. "If you stop saying your *namaz* regularly, you will get into trouble again," she warned me.

Domestic Disaster

Then one day my wife said, "Today is All Souls' Day and we have to go to the graveyard to burn incense, so come back early from work." I realized I was in real trouble now and didn't know how to get out of this one. But I replied, "I will take you to the graveyard but I will not enter in. You do whatever you need to but I will wait for you outside and take you home when you finish."

This raised her hackles at once. "What do you mean? Why will you not come inside with me? What is wrong with you? Why have you been behaving so strangely all this time?"

I was stuck now and had no choice but to tell her the truth because I was not prepared to disobey God and do something which was against his Word. So I told her, "I have accepted Jesus Christ as my Savior and I cannot follow all these rituals any more." She stared at me shocked, and then blurted out, "Are you out of your mind? Has that sister of yours finally done something to you and turned you around? I knew that one day she would try and convert you."

I hastened to the defence of my sister, "Safia *Apa* has nothing to do with this. She did not influence me in any way. I specifically asked God to show me the way and he did." I told her what had happened but she could not understand or accept this. She was too shocked to make any sense of my words, and continued to tell me that I was talking nonsense and that my sister must be the real cause of all this.

It was a horrible fight and our arguments went back and forth as I tried to convince her that it was my personal decision and that no one else was to blame. She refused to accept that. Finally I realized that this was not going to get me anywhere so I decided to follow the Bible's injunction to not argue needlessly, and I kept quiet. I had always known that I could not have continued following my faith secretly forever, and that a public confession would have to be made soon, but I had foolishly tried to postpone that day. After all, Jesus had said, "Whoever loves his father and mother and brothers and sisters and wife more than me cannot be my disciple." The time had finally come for me to take my stand.

But the following months were agony for me. There was a cold silence between my wife and I, and we lost our happy intimacy. A suppressed anger within her over the betrayal of my faith, and a hostile, unhappy atmosphere at home began affecting my children and me so much, that I almost contemplated going back to Islam for the sake of peace in the house. But the Lord Jesus sustained me and gave me grace to face the lonely persecution. After two months of living in this manner, my wife finally decided she could not take any more and left for her father's house with the children.

I was heartbroken. Was all this worth losing my family over? I struggled deep in my heart and then I turned to the Lord and said, "Lord, your Word says that we must believe in the Lord Jesus Christ and our family will be saved. But Lord, just the opposite of your Word has happened. My whole family has left me and gone. Oh God, what will happen to me? What about my wife and my sons? Please tell me what will happen to me, my wife and sons." I wept and wept and then went to sleep.

The next morning I opened my Bible for my morning devotion and the reading for that day was from the book of Psalms, chapter 128. As I read the first three verses, my spirit suddenly leaped, 1. "Blessed are all who fear the Lord, who walk in his ways. 2. You will eat the fruit of your labor; blessings and prosperity will be yours." Here the Lord was telling me I was going to be blessed and prosperous if I walk in his ways. But what about my wife?

Then I read verse 3. "Your wife will be like a fruitful vine within your house." I thought—what a wonderful promise! Right now my wife was not in my house, she was in her father's house, but the Lord had spoken and comforted me that someday she was going to be like a fruitful vine within my house. I needed faith to believe that. And what about my sons? I continued to read verse 3, "your sons will be like olive shoots around your table."

My wife and my sons! Just the previous night I had been crying out to the Lord and asking him what will happen to my wife and sons, and God had answered me directly from his Word. What a wonderful God! What a specific God! He didn't tell me what will happen to my sister or brother or business; he only spoke to me about my wife and sons!

I rushed to my sister and told her all that had happened and how the Lord had spoken to me from Psalm 128, and I asked her, "Is this God's promise for me? When will he fulfill it?" She nodded her head and said, 'Yes, I believe this is God's promise for you. I don't know when he will fulfill it, but he will, in his perfect time. He never goes back on his promise."

Even though my sister had confirmed my hope, I still had doubts in my mind. After all, my wife had left in such anger. How was God going to be able to touch her?

Suddenly I recalled the words Jesus had spoken in the Gospel of Matthew, "For I have come to turn a man against his father, a daughter against her mother, a daughter-in-law against her mother-in-law; a man's enemies will be the members of his own household." And it struck me that Jesus never said that he had come to separate husband from wife. So my spirits picked up a bit. I also remembered that God had said in the Scriptures, "Heaven and earth will pass away but my words will never pass away." That clinched my faith and I stood firm on this promise and believed that God would do a miracle in my wife's heart as well.

Restoration and Baptism

My faith was well rewarded. To my complete joy, just a few days later my wife returned home after an experience with God herself, and my family was complete again. Jesus Christ is always faithful to his Word, and just 3 months after I accepted the Lord, my wife gave her heart to the Lord Jesus Christ and asked him to become her personal Savior as well. God's promise was fulfilled in my wife's life. Praise the Lord! My sons have not come to him yet, but I believe that God will keep his promise concerning them as well. He will draw my boys to himself in his perfect time, and they will be like olive shoots around my table. He has said it. He will do it.

After my wife's conversion, we began attending a local church. My friend was the pastor and we began worshiping there regularly, growing strong in our faith and spiritual life. As we continued to read the Holy Scriptures, we realized that the Lord Jesus had commanded his followers to be baptized, so in May 1992, my wife and I were baptized by immersion and we were filled with greater joy as we walked in obedience to the Lord's will. It was a very spiritual experience for me as I put my old self to death by submerging myself under the water in, a symbolic act of burial; and as I emerged from the water, my soul felt clean and new. Resurrection from burial, life from death; it was truly a statement to the Powers of the Air that we belonged to the kingdom of God and that Jesus was our King now.

A Fresh Mandate

One day a thought floated into my mind that since God had given us such a big house, we should set aside two rooms for the worship of Jesus Christ. I didn't share this thought with anyone, not even my wife; I just kept it at the back of my mind. Two days later, my wife approached me and said she wanted to discuss some spiritual matter with me. When I asked her what it was, she said, "God has given us such a big house, why don't we set aside two rooms for the worship of Jesus Christ?" I was astounded as she spoke the same words that I had hidden in my heart the past two days. I knew at once that God's hand was in this.

We felt we needed further confirmation so we asked our sister who was like a spiritual mother to us by now, what she thought. She answered us, "Many years ago, the Lord had given me a vision that this whole place would become a church. I didn't dare tell anyone about it; I only prayed as the Lord led me to. I believe that this is definitely a word from the Lord."

But I wanted a direct confirmation from the Word of God as well, and that came when I was doing my morning devotions as I read from the book of Haggai, chapter one and verse 8 which stated, "Go up into the mountains and bring down timber and build the house so that I may take pleasure in it and be honoured, says the Lord." It was as though that verse just jumped out from the page and hit me in the face and I knew that the Lord was speaking to me.

There was yet another confirmation that came the next

Sunday as we worshiped in church. The preacher opened his Bible and told us to turn to the book of Haggai and he began to read, *"Go up into the mountains and bring down timber and build the house, so that I may take pleasure in it and be honored, says the LORD."* That was all the confirmation that we needed. There was no doubt in our minds now that God wanted us to begin building his house in our two rooms first. And that's what we set about doing.

It was a humble endeavor. We had no money to even renovate those two rooms, but when God asks us to do something for him, he always makes a way. The money came in miraculously and we soon started a regular English Service on Sunday. People began to flock in and soon there was standing room only; it was a very tight squeeze in our small rooms. I remember we did not even have a pulpit, so my wife would convert her sewing machine table into a temporary pulpit by pulling out the machine and placing a cardboard piece over the hole. That would double up as the Communion table as well.

We discovered that the Lord does not need fancy buildings or expensive furniture in which to be worshiped and honored. His main requirements are obedience and holiness. In those two tiny rooms with a sewing machine for a pulpit, God would come down and mingle with us. It was an awesome time of fellowship with the Almighty and his humble servants.

My business continued to be a draining liability which I needed to get rid of, so after much prayer and seeking of God's will on the matter, I sold it off. It was wonderful to see how God helped me clear my debts and loan completely. But now with the loan cleared and the business sold, I didn't know how I was supposed to provide for my wife and children.

So I asked the Lord, "Lord, what would you have me do now?" That morning I was reading in Ezekiel 33 when verse 7 stood out from the other verses, *"Son of man, I have made you a watchman for the house of Israel; so hear the word I speak and give them warning from me."* As I finished reading those words, God spoke to me directly, "I want you to preach to your countrymen and be a watchman to them."

I was stunned. Was I hearing God clearly and accurately? I reminded the Lord, "Lord, you remember my academic record, don't you? I'm not exactly preacher material and I stutter and get intimidated by those cleverer than I. How can you want me to preach to my countrymen? Who am I to speak to them? And how will I do that? Do you want me to leave my family all by themselves at home and go around preaching all over India?"

I was quite shaken by this mandate, but God knew my heart, that I would be willing to do whatever he wanted me to, so I yielded my will to his and waited to see how he would bring this about.

The Scripture says that God is not a man that he should lie. He is the Truth and he always speaks the truth. A few days later, I found some people from a well-known Radio organization waiting at my house with a proposal. They wanted me to be a speaker on their radio station and to preach the Word of God in Deccani Urdu! They had been searching for someone who could preach in this dialect and had been directed to my doorstep.

Oh, how mysterious are God's ways—how strangely he moves! God had said he wanted me to preach to my countrymen and when I questioned as to how that could be possible, he sent people from the radio broadcasting station to me with this proposal. Now, through this medium, I would be able to preach to my people all over the country. Nothing is ever complicated in God's scheme of things; it is only we who complicate issues. Knowing that this was God's will, I accepted their offer and began preaching over the air waves.

Church on the Roof

Then God spoke to my wife and me again that we should now build a church on the roof of our house. The problem of finance for this big project crept up again, and we wondered where so much money was going to come from? Once again we turned our eyes to our Provider. As we brought this up for prayer before the congregation, the Lord laid upon the heart of my brother-in- law, Ilyas Bhai, to give us an interest-free loan for the estimated sum. We assured him that we would be able to, by God's grace, pay him back all the money within 10 years. We prayed about this and felt peace in our heart, so we went ahead and soon our terrace had a big hall built on it dedicated to the worship of the Lord Jesus Christ. There were some days when even this hall could not hold all the people who used to come to hear the good news of salvation and to worship the Lord.

About a year later the Lord spoke to my wife and me, this time through a guest speaker at our church. After the service, he took me aside and said, "Vizarath, what are you doing? When I came in today I was expecting an Urdu service but was surprised to see that it was conducted in English. You are an Urdu speaking person; you should be conducting your service in Urdu."

I knew that he was speaking from the Lord because his words stabbed at my heart. My wife had all along been suggesting that I should also begin an Urdu service, but I had resisted her as our congregation was English speaking and we were doing so well. But now I knew I had to obey God who had resorted to sending a prophetic voice to shake me into action and so I announced to our congregation what we were planning to do. There were murmurs amongst the people who did not want any change, but we pressed in with God's desire.

Six weeks later, at our first Urdu service, there were only 6 people sitting in the church; my sister, her husband, my wife, me and two others. I was devastated. God had told me to start an Urdu service and nobody had come. We had lost a big congregation because they were not happy with the transition. I was told in no uncertain terms by an ex-member, "You have made a very big mistake."

I began to entertain doubts again. Was that really the voice of God I had heard, or had I missed him? I did not know then that when God gives a vision, he sometimes allows the vision to die before resurrecting it again. This way he gets all the glory and no man can claim victory by his own merit.

I ran the church this way for one whole year with only a handful of people attending. It was a terrible time for me and there were days when I would fall into a deep depression. But even though I was tempted to close down the church many times, I continued to persevere because the power and the anointing of God were still upon me, and his presence continued to abide with me.

My sister has testified that on the days when there was no congregation in the church, I must have preached in the presence of angels because she could feel waves of the anointing and presence of God so strongly in the hall. I knew that this was a time of testing to see if I would be completely obedient to his will, but I must confess there were times that I despaired. Gradually, however, the Lord began leading people back into his church and soon the hall began filling up again.

For 9 years we ran the church in this manner until God led us down a new road. I happened to attend some sessions on church planting and contextualization and it had a deep impact on my heart. God then began to lead me in the direction of converting our morning service to a contextualized one. I obeyed and I was amazed to see how the Muslim people as well as the Muslim converts liked this style of worship so much. It appealed to their sense of reverence and awe of God.

A Muslim who is accustomed to worshiping God reverently feels like a fish out of water when he is suddenly accosted by the western style of worship. A contextualized form of worship is the perfect setting to make him feel culturally comfortable in worshiping the Living God. So we began to have two services every Sunday. The morning one was contextualized and completely in Urdu and the evening one was in English.

What a long way the Lord has brought us. We were just two simple Muslims, completely unaware of his love and grace and he made us pastors of his church with the divine privilege of feeding his sheep. He took our two fish and five loaves and multiplied them to nurture and sustain the many that came to our little church. From the two small rooms that we offered him, he allowed us to build a hall to worship his name. I was looking for more people in my church; he was looking for Christ to be formed in me. Praise the Lord.

Being the inveterate preacher that I am, may I take the liberty of summing up this testimony to bless you with ten points of encouragement?

God has a purpose for our lives

There was no earthly reason for me to live as I was given up for dead. But God had a purpose for my life and that was to give me the gift of salvation when I was 38 years old, to forgive my sins through the blood of Jesus Christ, to be the minister and pastor of a church and to bring glory to his name.

In Psalm 57, verse 2, David says, *I cry out to God Most High, to God who fulfills his purpose for me.* David had been chased by Saul and had to flee for his life from him, but God's purpose was that David would become the king of Israel and he fulfilled that purpose for him. Philippians chapter 1, verse 6 says, "Being confident of this, that he who began a good work in you will carry it on to completion until the day of Christ Jesus."

God's purpose is not hindered by our failures

God does not consider our failures. He does not look at our intelligence, our weaknesses or our inadequacy. I was a total failure in school. I repeated several classes in school and in college and I was a failure in business. That did not stop God from working in my life. He set aside my failures and started working in me through his strength. That is why the apostle Paul said, "When I am weak, then I am strong." It is God's strength that works in our weakness.

The apostle Peter was initially quite a failure; he was brash and impulsive and he even denied Jesus three times. But his failures didn't prevent God from working in his life. He ultimately became the recognized leader of the disciples and was the first great voice of the gospel during and after Pentecost. He wrote two letters in the Bible and God used him mightily in signs and wonders.

God uses miracles to draw us to himself

As a Muslim, I was never close to God. Even though I had practiced so many rituals, I never really knew God and none of those rituals drew me close to him. But when the Pentecostal brother prayed for my sons at my sister's home and God healed them, that miracle certainly brought me closer to God. When I was threatened on the phone and after the prayer of my sister, no one troubled us any more, that miracle brought us closer to God. Only after the miracles did I begin to take refuge in God and trust in him for protection and ultimately for salvation.

God can turn evil into good

The threatening call that I received was an evil action that God used to prompt me to begin searching diligently for the truth, which ultimately led to my salvation. In the book of Genesis, we are told how Joseph's brothers were so jealous of him that they sold him into slavery. Joseph lived a hard life in Egypt, even suffering unjust accusations from Potiphar's wife and being thrown into jail. But in spite off all his sufferings, God finally made him Prime Minister of all Egypt. In Genesis 50: 19-20, Joseph said to his brothers, "Don't be afraid. Am I in the place of God? You intended to harm me but God intended it for good to accomplish what is now being done, the saving of many lives."

God cannot be found through religion

The more religious I became and the more I followed all the rituals and read all the books in my search for God, the more distant he became. The Gospels tell us that the Pharisees were very religious people. They used to follow the law and practice every ritual and were very proud of their righteousness. They were so blinded by their own knowledge that when Jesus performed a miracle of opening blind eyes in front of them, they could not believe or understand.

John 9:28-34 says,

Then they hurled insults at him and said, "You are this fellow's disciple! We are disciples of Moses! We know that God spoke to Moses, but as for this fellow, we don't even know where he comes from." The man answered, "Now that is remarkable! You don't know where he comes from, yet he opened my eyes. We know that God doesn't listen to sinners. He listens to the godly man who does his will. Nobody has ever heard of opening the eyes of a man born blind. If this man were not from God he could do nothing." To this they replied, "You were steeped in sin at birth: how dare you lecture us!" And they threw him out.

The religiosity of the Pharisees made it impossible for them to seek God.

God answers heartfelt prayers

When I used to say my Namaz, I was not praying for my salvation because I could not understand the Arabic words I was speaking. I didn't even know the meaning of salvation. When I prayed in my mother tongue and asked God to reveal the right way to me, he answered my question specifically and revealed to me that Jesus was the only way to heaven, and not any religion.

Accepting Jesus brings persecution

Always and definitely! It was very difficult for me when my wife rejected me and my beliefs after my conversion, and I was so unhappy and confused until I read in Luke 12: 51-53 where Jesus says,

"Do you think I came to bring peace on earth? No, I tell you, but division. From now on, there will be five in one family divided against each other, three against two and two against three. They will be divided, father against son and son against father, mother against daughter and daughter against mother, mother-in-law against daughter-in-law and daughter-in-law against mother-in-law."

God always keeps his promise

When I was weeping before the Lord for my wife and sons, God gave me a promise from Psalm 128:3, *Your wife will be like a fruitful vine within your house; and your sons will be like olive shoots around your table.* God kept his promise and my wife certainly became like a fruitful vine. Today she helps me in my ministry, my church and my home. Whatever I want to do, she is always there to support me.

In Psalm 145:13, David says about God, *Your kingdom is an everlasting kingdom and your dominion endures through all generations. The LORD is faithful to all his promises and loving towards all he has made.*

God uses the weak to shame the strong

I was born weak in health, in academics and in business, in speech and in every area of my life. But God has used me and is still using me to shame the strong and glorify his name. He picked up this weak vessel and raised him to be a minister, not of a nation but a minister in his kingdom.

1 Corinthians 1:27-29 says, *"But God chose the foolish things of the world to shame the wise, God chose the weak things of the world to shame the strong, he chose the lowly things of the world, and the despised things and the things that are not, to nullify the things that are, so that no one may boast before Him."*

The Lord Jesus Christ is the only way to heaven

In this world there is no one who can take us to heaven—no great religious leader, no great religious scholar, no great pious man. It is only the Lord Jesus Christ who says in John 14:6, *"I am the way and the truth and the life. No one comes to the Father except through me."* Jesus can take us to heaven, because he has come from heaven.

I have finally found meaning and purpose to my life. I have learned to be content in whatever situation because his word of promise to me is, "He will never leave me nor forsake me."

4

$\mathcal{A}$ Suitable Help Meet
Lateef's Testimony

By the time August rolls around in Hyderabad, the monsoon season is generally in full swing. The months before would have ensured that the summer sun had baked the fields to a sweltering crisp; but with the advent of the monsoon rains, all that is reduced to a dim memory. Lush greenery abounds and the earthy scent of wet mud fills the air, along with the perfume of jasmine and frangipani.

In such a month of the year 1957, I was born into a conservative Shia Muslim family in the city of Hyderabad. Traditionally, Indian parents crave a boy as their first born, but I was welcomed with open arms and much rejoicing by my parents. They did not mind having a girl and were grateful to Allah for a healthy child. They figured there would be many more opportunities to have a boy later on and they were right. I was blessed with three more siblings in life, of which two were brothers.

The moment I was born, my family recorded the time, the day and the date of my birth and after all the necessary astrological calculations, one of the elders in my family selected the alphabet my name should begin with. It was the letter L, and so my parents named me Lateefunissa.

We were a very loving and close knit family. As the eldest, I was responsible for looking after my siblings and cousins since we all lived in a joint family, the norm in those days. Our childhood was spent chasing each other through the narrow gullies of the old city, dodging all the swarming people and traffic. As expected in our culture, my parents were concerned about me becoming modern, so even though I was sent to study in an English medium school called Mehboobia, it was practically like studying at home. The majority of the students were Muslims and I remember that we girls had to go to school in a rickshaw covered with purdah (veil). Even entering the school was done in a veiled manner, with the passageway flanked with bed sheets as we quickly filed inside.

I was extremely religious even from childhood, loving my faith and my prophet with a quiet yet intense fervor. I learnt the salat at a young age and prayed it without fail 5 times a day. I would also faithfully fast every Ramadan and take active part in all the religious festivals. Aside from the regular *ustad,* or spiritual teacher, my grandmother would teach us children about other spiritual matters, and she trained us to be so religious that we had to recite some particular scriptures even before switching on a light!

A morbid fascination with all the meaningful rituals performed during Muharram also enthralled me. I would wear the black clothes of mourning and beat my chest during the *majlis* (the special gathering in remembrance of the Prophet's grandson). This *taziya,* or passion play commemorating the martyrdom of the third Imam Hussein, served to identify us with his great sacrifice for the cause of Islam. On one of the days of Muharram, I would also carry the alam, a pole bearing the insignia of the Hand, and run barefooted on a carpet of hot coals, just to show my devotion to the Imam. My feet never got scalded or charred on the burning coals. Truly, religious euphoria can overcome even the confines of physical limitations.

This ardent devotion to Allah earned me the reputation of being God's favored pet. Some of my religious and pious elders believed that if I asked God for any favor he would grant it to me, so requests for my intercession flooded in, with promises of much recompense if their petitions were answered.

But my greatest joy lay in reciting the 99 names of Allah over and over again at least once every day. I was particularly partial to the attribute of God from which my name was derived; Ya Lateefo, *Allah*—the gracious one, and I would repeat this name 129 times on my prayer beads, the *tazbi*. Why that number? Because the numerical significance of the letters in my name added up to that number, which was considered auspicious in itself.

Marriage Prospects

My mother desired that I continue with my education after High School, so I was allowed to study two more years before matrimonial prospects were considered. I had some fears and hesitation about marriage, and I used to pray and hope that if it was Allah's will he would let me be married to a good husband, a man who would respect me and love me. I didn't hanker after riches or fame; I just wanted a good man who would take care of me and for us to be happy. I had been somewhat disillusioned by a few failed marriages around me and was scared of the same fate. What if I too got a man who didn't love or treat me well? What if he was harsh to our children or if he married many wives? Suppose he divorced me, how would I bear the shame? These thoughts used to plague me a lot and I was very apprehensive.

One day my aunt invited me to her house for a visit. I did

not know that she was setting me up for a meeting involving a marriage proposal, so when I went over to her house and saw that she still had some incomplete household chores left to do, I set about helping her finish them. As I was washing the dirty vessels, my aunt's cousin Safia *Apa* walked in to her house and we were introduced to each other. I was not really dressed for company, in fact I was looking quite scruffy after all the cleaning I had been doing. But she didn't seem to mind, and seemed a pleasant enough person, even though I had heard whispered stories among my relatives about her conversion to Christianity.

I thought nothing of that meeting until a few days later when I was informed that her family had sent a proposal to me for her youngest brother Vizarath. I was quite surprised. What had his sister seen in me that day to ask for my hand in marriage? I had certainly not dressed for the occasion and we had barely exchanged a few words. Much discussion followed among my family members whether this proposal should be accepted or not, with the majority not in favor of it. But even with so many against this alliance, the *nikaah* (solemnizing) ceremony still went through and I was married to Vizarath on October 6, 1980. It must have been the will of Allah in answer to my prayer.

I was very happy with my new husband. He was extremely gentle and caring, and there was an element of fragility in him which appealed to me and made me want to nurture him. He was not very robust physically but then, neither was I, so we were patient and sympathetic with each others' weaknesses. My new family was good as well and it was not difficult making this transition into marital life.

It was only much later that I asked my sister-in-law, "Safia *Apa* (big sister) what made you choose me for your brother that day when you met me in your cousin's house?" Her reply was nothing that I could have imagined.

She said, "I was most unsure of myself and not at all confident about making the right choice, so I simply prayed to my God and told him, 'God, You know the beginning from the end. The future is in your hands. Only you know whether this girl will be the right choice, not only for my brother but for our whole family. After all, she has to be the one to adjust to our way of living, especially with me being a Christian. I don't want there to be any friction between her and me which will result in my brother being torn between the two of us.

"So I am asking you for a sign. If she is the right girl for my brother, then let her be dressed very simply and let her be doing some household chores when I meet her. If she is not sitting there decked out in fine clothes, then I will take it as a sign from you that she is your choice."

I was surprised and a bit flattered as well. However, that did not stop me from making sure that I kept a safe distance between my sister-in-law's family and mine. Even though we shared the same house, I did not want too much of her Christian influence around me and my children.

Healing Received

I got pregnant in the first year of marriage and everything was going smoothly with the pregnancy until I slipped in the bathroom and landed heavily on the floor. After that, complications began to surface. The baby took a cross position in my womb and the umbilical cord got wound around his throat. The doctor advised an immediate Caesarean section and my son was delivered safely in a Catholic Nursing Home, but both of us were in a very serious condition. The nuns and nurses there told my mother that she should offer thanks and money to Mother Mary who had helped me with a safe delivery, so she did. It is not uncommon for

Muslims to revere Mary as there is a full chapter in the Koran dedicated to her.

However, my body rejected the nylon sutures that had been used to stitch me up and the wound refused to heal. It got septic and dripped constantly and I began to get weaker and frailer. It was agony trying to look after my baby boy. When there was no healing after four months, another surgery was done on me but again the sutures did not heal, so we began to make the rounds to all the *mullahs* in the city, seeking healing from spiritual sources. One of them even wrote verses from the Koran on my abdomen with saffron, an herb which is considered efficacious for good health and healing. Such a potent combination of natural and spiritual medicine should have worked but it didn't.

After suffering in agony for 15 months, some of the elders in my family advised us to make a pilgrimage to a place in Madhya Pradesh called Jawrah which was supposed to be a center for spiritual and physical healing. Many people possessed by demons were reputed to have been set free there as well. The shrine was dedicated to Hazrat Abbas, one of the sons of Imam Hazrat Ali and was reputed to have miraculous powers.

My husband and I decided to go. We thought if we made the right offerings at this shrine, surely we would be delivered of this physical suffering. After completing all the rituals there, we came home expecting that healing would soon follow. But no such thing happened and the festering and the oozing continued for 5 more months till I developed a high fever and was admitted back to the same Nursing Home. This time however, the doctor who had assured me that I would be healed by her treatment just washed her hands off the case and left me there in my misery.

My husband and family were in deep despair as they surrounded my hospital bed expecting the worst at any moment. They all thought that I would not be able to survive as I was almost comatose, drifting in and out of a painful haze. My husband called my sister in law Safia *Apa* and gave her the news of my serious condition. She asked if he would allow her friend Madhubala to pray for me and he agreed, so they both came down to my room in the hospital to pray for healing; when my family saw them and realized their intentions, they walked out.

Safia *Apa* and Madhubala then proceeded to make me recite some prayer which I now know is called the sinner's prayer. I had no idea what I was repeating after them as I was in such a drowsy state; I only remember quite vaguely repenting of my sins to Jesus Christ and asking him to come into my heart. There was no understanding or conviction from my side, just a sense of obligation within me that since they had come in such compassion to pray for me, the least I could do was cooperate with them.

They then prayed a simple prayer asking Jesus to heal me completely, and as soon as they finished saying, "in Jesus' name, Amen"; almost instantly, my fever left me and I was fresh and alert again. Without any medication given to me, I felt new strength flowing into my body. It was nothing short of a miracle. There was no further need for me to stay in the hospital any more and I got up and we went home. In a short while my wound healed up and there was no more oozing, after almost 20 months of constant infection.

But did I attribute this miracle to Jesus and give him thanks for it? Not at all. When I look back on my life now, I realize how blind I had been to all that the Lord was doing for me; first in giving a sign to Safia *Apa* that I was to be chosen for their family, and then this miracle of healing. Jesus Christ came into this world to open the eyes of the blind and to set the captives free, but it is we who must allow him to do it first. I just carried on with my life, ignoring all these signposts of God's grace.

Healing Needed Again

And then my baby developed asthma and our world fell apart. He became such a sickly child that every two weeks we had to rush him to the doctor. His labored breathing used to be so loud; they could hear him wheezing in the adjoining house. Can you imagine what it is like for a mother to watch her precious child struggle for every breath of air?

I would cry out to Allah, "O Allah, have mercy and heal my child. Forgive me if I have brought this calamity upon us because I have not been praying enough to you." My times of prayer had certainly lessened, firstly, because I had been unclean due to my oozing all these months and, secondly, looking after the baby tired me out immensely as well. So I felt that God was probably angry with us for not saying the *namaz* (salat) and worshiping him, and so he was punishing us now.

The doctor's clinic where I used to take my son was about 10 km away and I would sometimes have to go there in the late evenings when his clinic would be open. The ride there would be quite dark most of the time, and sitting in the auto rickshaw with my sick son, I would keep up a constant recitation of prayer throughout.

We had to drive over a railway crossing on the way to the doctor, and there was a wall alongside, on which I would notice a painted sign of bold letters which read JESUS CHRIST HEALS YOU. Somehow it seemed as though the dim street lights would illuminate that brightly for my benefit only, and reading it always gave me an element of comfort. I would think of how I myself had been healed after so many months of suffering, and those words always gave me a strange assurance that my boy would also be healed some day.

Our second son was born 7 years later and he also turned out to be as sickly as the first, suffering with asthma and many other allergies as well. We would pray so desperately, going to every *dargah*, *mazar* and *moulana*, tying so many talismans on the children, but to no avail.

One day, my sister-in-law, Safia *Apa*, who used to feel great compassion for my sons, called my husband to her side and asked him if he would be willing to bring the boys over to her house that afternoon. She told him that some man of God was having lunch with them and if he wanted, she would ask him to pray for the boys' healing.

Vizarath came home and asked me what I thought we should do. I told him, "If you want, you can take your sons there but I will not come with you. I feel uncomfortable in their Christian meetings. But you please be careful and stay alert. I don't want you to be mesmerized by this man and have you come back home a Christian like your sister."

They returned a short while later and I checked carefully to see whether they had been affected in any way. I asked my husband what had happened there but he just answered me briefly, giving no details, so I kept a strict watch on the boys myself. After a few days I noticed something strange. Gone was their labored and heavy breathing. Gone was their weak and sickly demeanor. They seemed to have been healed of asthma completely. I didn't need to make my fortnightly visit to the doctor any more. What a blessing, what a relief, yet even with that, I was reluctant to give Jesus Christ all the credit for their healing.

My mother passed away soon after and I began visiting my father more often to help look after his needs. Vizarath supported me in this and never objected to my division of duty. He helped me with everything and we were very united in doing things together. One day we received a wedding invitation to attend my cousin's wedding in Mysore, and I was excited about going there with my family, but strangely enough, this was the first time that my husband didn't want to go with me. He made some excuse about work and told me to take our sons and go by myself.

After my return from the wedding, I began to sense a change in Vizarath. I couldn't put my finger on it, but he was not the same man that I had left behind. One day the children missed their school bus and I called Vizarath in the printing press. But he was not there and his workers said that he had come to the office but had gone out again, and nobody knew where he was.

This was extremely strange and unlike him. I was surprised but when I questioned his whereabouts, he just evaded me and wouldn't give me a straight answer. I got very upset and threatened him that if he was not upfront with me, I would go to my parents house. Suddenly the solid relationship that we had shared all these years seemed to be getting a bit shaky and I did not like it. We were almost turning into strangers.

The final straw came when I reminded him that we needed to go to the cemetery on All Soul's Day to pray for our ancestor's souls. He turned around and flatly refused to accompany me. In great shock, I spoke out, "What do you mean you will not come with me? What has gone wrong with you Vizarath? You have changed somehow and I don't like the change. We have always gone every year together to the cemetery. Why do you not want to come with me this year?"

I kept pestering him for an answer. Finally he blurted out, "I cannot come with you to the cemetery because I have accepted Jesus Christ as my Lord and Savior."

For a moment it felt like I had been suspended in mid-air and all external sound had ceased, except these words which kept thundering loudly—"I have accepted Jesus, I have accepted Jesus" and then all the noise came back with a vengeance, and I felt like there was an earthquake in my soul. Anger began to well up within me, as well as hatred, loathing and betrayal. I was overwhelmed with all these alien emotions and suddenly I could not stand to even look at him.

How could he have done this to me? How could he leave his faith and betray us all? There was no way now that I could live with an infidel. My religion would not allow it. I was very upset and very angry.

"Listen to me Vizarath," I said, "I am taking my children and going back to my father's house. If you continue to be a traitor to our religion, I will not allow my children to be influenced and corrupted by you. I married you a Muslim, and if you are no longer the man I married, then I cannot live with you anymore."

I knew that I had hurt my husband very much. He loved me and our children and I could see that he was very upset with my decision. He tried his best to make me change my mind, but I was adamant. To be fair, I did attempt to go back and live with him again after he begged me repeatedly, but each time we would end up quarrelling bitterly and I would once again return to my father's house.

Finally I told him that if he wanted me home he would have to stop going for his prayer meetings. I would not object if he read his Bible while I was doing my *namaz*, but that was as far as it would go. So, for the sake of our sons, we did try to adjust to this new development, but even with that compromise, I found I could not live with a non-Muslim in the house any more and I left for the final time. My heart was filled with much bitterness against him.

I was extremely unhappy. No woman ever wants to deliberately break up her home. So I went to a *maulvi* and told him my whole predicament, hoping that his prayers and advice would help the situation, but after listening to me, he just casually told me that all I could do was pray and intercede to God. That hardly seemed like very impressive advice and I left him feeling disheartened and dejected. A wave of great rejection and hurt washed over me as I suddenly felt all alone in the world. I felt as though there was not a single person who could help me and the future looked very dark and bleak for me and my children. However, I decided to take the *maulvi's* advice to pray.

I went home, did all my ritual purification, the *wudu*, washed my face and hands, got my prayer mat out, knelt on it and then dissolved into tears. It was the time of the afternoon *namaz*, the *zohar*, and from then till the evening *isha ki namaz*, (sunset prayer), I wept and prayed continuously. My tears formed a river on my prayer mat as I beseeched Allah to bring my husband back to the true faith once again. I began to speak and cry out to God in my own language Urdu.

Previously I had just recited scripted prayers, but this time I cried out to God in my own tongue and I asked him, "Why is all this happening to me? Why is my whole world falling apart? Why must my children have to suffer like this? O Allah, since a young age, I have always been so devoted to you, so faithful in all my religious activities. I have loved reciting your beautiful names. I loved meditating on your grace. I always asked for your grace. But where is that grace now? Why is there such darkness in my life? What have I done to deserve this? How will I face the shame of divorce in my life?"

As the tears continued to flow down the mat on which I was prostrated, a thought suddenly occurred to me that maybe I should appeal to the Prophet *Isa* also and see whether he would be able to help me with this problem. After all, I reckoned, we considered him a prophet of high ranking too, so it should be all right to enlist his help as well. So I told him, "Hazrat Isa, I know you are a very great prophet. But now my world is so full of darkness and I cannot see any light for the future. My children's future looks so bleak as well. What hope is there for me without a husband? Can you help me once again?"

God's Answer

I badly needed a sign from God that he was listening to my frantic prayers. What if I was just wasting my time crying out to him and he was not even listening to me? So I said to Allah, "O merciful and gracious Allah, please give me a sign that your ears are tuned to my cries, and that you are hearing me. My wisdom is very limited, only you are All-Wise. Please speak to me clearly, and give me a sign that you are hearing and will answer my prayers and petitions. I need to know that it is you alone who are guiding me. Please give me a sign of your graciousness."

As I lifted my head off the mat, my attention was suddenly distracted by a movement from the round ventilation shaft on the wall in front of me. As I looked up, two beautiful white birds that had been perched on it flew towards me, over my head and went to the back of the room, perching on the grill of the door behind. They seemed to be looking intently at me as though trying to convey some message and as I stared back at them, the first question that came to my mind was, "God are these your angels who are carrying my prayers up to you?"

As a strange joy began to bubble up within me, I heard a voice very clearly within my heart say, "You are not alone. I am with you. What you have asked for, you will receive and much more as well, for it will be an abundant treasure. You are not in darkness. Jesus is your light. Jesus is not merely a prophet; he is more than a prophet."

As I heard these words in my spirit, I felt a load lift off my back and all my fears, anger and insecurity just dissipated. Jesus was more than a prophet? Who could be more than a prophet? Only God was higher than a prophet. Had I misunderstood who Isa was all these years? Could my husband and sister-in-law actually be right?

All this while I had been adamant about my decision to not return to my husband, but now there was such a change in my heart that I felt like I would burst if I didn't share this experience with Vizarath. The desire to run home right then became almost unbearable. It was like a force propelling me, but the problem was that it was late at night and there was no way a lone woman could go out by herself.

So I waited for my brother to return home and then I asked him to take me to my husband that very minute. He looked at me as though I had gone crazy and reminded me that the children were sleeping and it was late. He promised to take me first thing the next morning, but I was compelled to go now and confess to my husband what had happened. There was no one at home that I could share this beautiful experience and revelation with in my father's house. They would have probably thought I had gone mad with the stress of my marriage. So I continued to pester my brother until grumbling, he finally agreed to take me back.

When I arrived home, I found all the lights on. My husband was awake. I rang the bell and when he opened the door and saw me, he was very surprised to see me there at that time of the night and without the children as well. I could see his sad face etched with tears of sorrow and realized that he had been suffering as much as me. I came straight to the point and asked him, "Vizarath, is it true that Jesus really is the Light?"

Vizarath realized at once that something significant had happened to me, but since he was such a young Christian himself, he knew he wouldn't be able to help me by himself, so he ran and woke up his sister to answer my doubts. Tears were flowing down all our faces as we realized that God was at work.

I asked Safia *Apa*, "Is it true that Jesus really is the Light?

Safia *Apa* simply put a New Testament in my hand and opened it to John 9:5 where Jesus says, "I am the Light of the world."I began to flip open the pages. I was still struggling and finding it difficult to accept everything about Jesus, because the opposite had been so deeply ingrained in me for so long.

As I flipped open the Bible at random, it opened to John 1: 1-5 and as I began to read it, each verse seemed to answer every doubt of mine.

In the beginning was the Word, and the Word was with God and the Word was God. He was with God in the beginning. Through him all things were made; without him nothing was made that has been made. In him was life, and that life was the light of men. The light shines in the darkness, but the darkness has not understood it.

This was incredible. I had asked the man I considered as the prophet *Isa* to show me some light in my dark world and this was what the Bible was saying about him. He was life and light!

The words I was reading and the emotions I was experiencing became all jumbled up in each other and I found myself weeping in repentance and regret, telling God, "How can I, who have rejected you so continuously, receive your forgiveness? I, who was never willing to listen to anyone about Jesus, how can you make use of me and what can I ever do for you? How could you show me such grace, when I was so hard hearted towards you? You are such a great God, how can you stoop down from so high and answer my prayers?"

As I continued to read from the book of John, suddenly the words from chapter 15, verse 16 shot out at me, *"You did not choose me, but I chose you and appointed you to go and bear fruit— fruit that will last."*

Last Defence Down

That was my last defence down. I quietly bowed my head and surrendered my life completely into Jesus' hands now. Much later I came to know that God had given this very promise from Psalm 128 to my husband that I would be a fruitful vine in his house. Praise the Lord!

As expected, there was much opposition from my family. They were completely staggered by this turn of events. They could not imagine that I, the one who was the most religious among them, the most devout of them all, had succumbed to this foolhardy deception. My aunts and uncles shut their door in my face. I was an outcast now and not welcome in their homes. It was a heartbreaking experience but the love of God strengthened me.

My youngest brother, who was very close to me, was the most shattered. He would plead and plead with me to return to Islam and not be foolish. But I stood firm in my faith. I had experienced the grace of God and never wanted to lose it again. I had regained my family in a stronger bond of love and unity; that was the next best thing after experiencing the love of God the Father. But even though I was an outcast to them, even though we faced our fair share of ridicule and abuse, it did not stop me from boldly witnessing for Jesus.

Baptism

As Vizarath and I continued to read God's Word together and grow in our faith, we came across Jesus' command to be baptized. Vizarath's pastor friend who had been discipling him since the past six months also encouraged us to get baptized, and so, in the heat of summer, on the 10th of May, that's what we did. We had such an intense desire to obey the Lord that even the scorching sun did not deter us from being baptized in the warm waters of the big tank at the Methodist Church. As we were first immersed and then lifted out of the water, I could actually feel a cleansing not only in my body but in my soul as well.

The fire of God anointed us with much boldness to continue to live for him and his purpose for our lives. In me he placed a deep burden and desire to share the good news with anyone I came in contact with, be it the plumber, the electrician or the milk man. Whomever I met, I would be sure to place a tract in their hand and share the love of the Lord with them. It was an exciting and fulfilling time. We didn't know from which side we would face danger and threat to our lives, but the Lord was faithful and protected us.

I was very drawn towards the ministry of mercy. My husband I would visit the hospital and as the Holy Spirit would lead us, we would enquire about the health of the patient and then offer to pray for healing in Jesus name. Sometimes they would reject the offer, but more often than not, they would welcome it. We would also visit the homes of old sick people who were unable to come to church and serve the Communion to them.

Healing Grace

In 2006, for all that the Lord was doing in and through my husband and me, we felt the attacks of the evil one from all sides. The worst one came in the month of October when I suddenly began to have a low grade fever with constant stomach aches. By the beginning of November, that changed to a high fever of 104 degrees every day. With all the medicines I was taking, it just wouldn't come down. Finally we got a complete blood analysis done and it was discovered that my white blood cell count was steadily falling. It should have been a minimum of 4000, but it had fallen to 1100.

The specialist thought I had an auto-immune disease which was incurable. We were heartbroken and looked to the Lord for help. I wanted him to save my life because I wanted to serve him more. But after moving from one hospital to another and finding no treatment, I was sent home without medication because there was none to give. With such a low count of white blood corpuscles what chance was there of survival? I was told that I had to be kept in a disinfected room which is impossible in India because infection is everywhere; in the air, the water and the food.

On returning home, Safia *Apa* told my husband, "Now, enough of hospitals and doctors. No more medicines. We are going to resort to intensive prayer therapy. Only prayer can heal her now."

Safia *Apa* also sought the Lord for confirmation from his Word whether or not the prayer therapy would work. The next day in her morning devotions, the Lord gave her a passage from Hosea 6:1. She read, *"Come let us return to the LORD. He has torn us to pieces but he will heal us; he has injured us but he will bind up our wounds. After two days he will revive us; on the third day he will restore us."* That was all the confirmation she needed.

The praying then began in real earnest and requests for intercession went out to different parts of the world as well. My family began praying for every cell and organ in my body, especially my enlarged spleen. They prayed over me from my head to my toe, asking the Holy Spirit to move over me with his healing power. They rebuked the attack of the demonic powers, speaking to my illness to leave, my spleen to reduce in size and my WBC count to rise. We claimed healing and total recovery in Jesus' name while thanking and praising him continuously for the promise of healing in his Word.

For 2 days I continued to have fever, but like God promised from Hosea 6, after those 2 days, everything was back to normal. The fever left my body and, true to the Word, on the third day, I walked up the staircase of the church to worship and thank

God on my own. We didn't need disinfectant from bacteria, we just needed the disinfectant of the blood of Christ, which washes away our sins and heals our diseases.

Since that day, I have become stronger physically as well as spiritually. Who can ever deny the power of this mighty God we serve? He has been my salvation, my comfort and my strength, protecting me from danger and harm; revealing to me his great love and mercy. I just want to praise and thank my Master for drawing me to his side, even when I was unwilling to go there.

My heart's desire is to see my people come to the realization of his great mercy and truth and to know for certain that it is only through Jesus that their sins can be forgiven and a place in heaven reserved for them.

Yet to all who received him, to those who believed in his name, he gave the right to become children of God (John 1:12).

May the Holy Spirit open the eyes of those from whom this truth has been veiled and who are blinded as I had been, and may his light shine in the darkness, bringing illumination to the very eyes of their hearts.

5

*B*ehind the Scenes
Athena's Musings

The first time I ever set eyes on Safia was in the 9th grade classroom at St. Ann's High School. I knew her as Mrs. Mirza. She had walked in briskly and had planted herself in front of the blackboard waiting for us all to settle down so she could begin teaching us History. She didn't have long to wait. There was something in the steely glint of her eyes and the tilt of her head that extinguished any desire in us to continue with our teenage raucousness. Swift silence descended immediately and everyone found their places and books quietly and quickly. Only then did she proceed to educate and enlighten us on the prosperous era of the Mughal Dynasty.

This was a woman who commanded immediate respect from those around her. She had an air of aloof Persian aristocracy which kept us all at a respectable distance, but no one could deny that she made the past come excitingly alive when she began to teach. As a young student in High School I was in complete awe of her, and was careful to do nothing that would incur her displeasure.

She had a lethally sharp tongue and though I towered over her in size even then, one displeased look from her was enough to reduce me to a small pile of ash.

Time moved on and so did I, as I followed first my father, and then my husband to wherever their professions led them. It was only about two decades later when I was visiting my retired parents in Hyderabad that I heard the astounding news that Mrs.Mirza had, of all things, become a Christian! I refused to believe my Muslim classmate who broke the news to me. To convince me and make me believe that she was not joking, she took me straight to her house to check it out for myself.

When we arrived there, we saw Mrs.Mirza standing at the doorstep of her house, almost as though she was expecting us. I felt a sudden twinge of trepidation as I alighted from the scooter, wondering if she would remember me after all these years, and what caustic comments she would make regarding my present matronly appearance. But my fears were unfounded. The moment she saw me, she squealed out my name in surprised recognition and enveloped me in a bear hug.

I was shocked out of my socks! Who was this warm, demonstrative, honey-eyed woman who was embracing me with such love? Had we come to the correct address? Physically, she looked exactly like the Mrs.Mirza of the past—there was no physical change in her at all—but this unusual warmth and affection flummoxed me completely.

It took a while for me to digest this cataclysmic change in her. As questions poured forth from my mouth, she graciously shared her story with me and, because I had experienced an abundant outpouring of grace from the Lord Jesus in my own life, I was able to comprehend and rejoice with her as we glorified God together for his goodness to both of us.

This unexpected reunion after all these years was certainly

no coincidence in my opinion, and definitely not the result of my curiosity alone. I believe it was a divinely orchestrated plan in God's perfect timetable in which he used Mrs. Mirza to impact my own life first. She was instrumental in praying and fasting for my husband and I to have a strong marriage in the Lord and soon after, dedicated our first daughter and third child to him. The love and bond that developed between us over the years strengthened steadily until she finally gave me this privilege of sharing her family's testimony with the rest of the world.

It is a powerful and encouraging testimony in that it has stood the test of time. The Christian life is not a short 100 meters dash; it is a long-distance marathon; and the fact that at the beginning of the race she was denied even the refreshing water that all marathon runners are entitled to along their route, must have made it doubly difficult for her to endure and persevere.

For ten long years she waited in the background, in complete submission to her husband's will, praying ceaselessly for the salvation of her loved ones. She had no recourse to cell groups and prayer meetings and worship services which we all take so casually for granted sometimes. It was just she and the Lord in the confines of her house where she continuously received the treasures of darkness and the riches stored in secret places. (Isaiah 45:3) and he faithfully sustained her by nourishing her of himself—as the Bread of Life and the Living Water.

Yet, even so, such an existence might have broken and swayed anyone less spiritually stalwart than she. In a world where marriages, relationships and even godly commitments crumble at the drop of a hat; where anything is acceptable and justified by a soft-peddling, seeker-sensitive gospel; where the fear of the Lord is only an academic biblical phrase to most people, Safia clung to the memory of how God had turned her world upside down with a divine mandate. The purpose of that heavenly touch was to strengthen her for the difficult times ahead, and to help her remain loyal and faithful to that calling.

This is why it is so vital for the disciple of Christ to have a true conversion and a real encounter with the Spirit of God. It does not have to resemble any one else's experience; the previous testimonies in this book reveal and prove how versatile God is in calling men to himself. It is not about these four people's experiences—it is all about the grace of an Almighty Powerful God and the working of his Holy Spirit—this mighty Spirit who cannot be confined or moulded into a box of any theological shape or size.

It is by the gentle yet convicting power of the Holy Spirit that we are enabled to see the Lord high and lifted up seated on the throne of his glory. It is only when we are able to see how high he is, that we can see the lowliness of our own depravity (Isaiah 6). Without that glimpse of his awesome glory, it is almost impossible to partake in the fellowship of his sufferings. Without that lump of burning coal from his temple cleansing our lips and lighting a fire in our spirits, we can only be on the track of that lukewarm life Jesus warned us against. Do we really want him to spit us out of his mouth? (Revelation 3:16).

I realize that there may be many out there who will not be able to understand or accept the sequence in which God, in his infinite wisdom and mercy, drew this family to himself. This route did not adhere to the standard evangelical pattern of raising one's hand in a meeting to accept the Lord, of repeating a prayer inviting the Lord Jesus to come into one's heart and then continuing pretty much in the same mode of life, with no inward or outward manifestation of a life-changing encounter.

For this family, it was a life and death struggle in just comprehending what God was trying to do; after coming to terms with the fact that here was a God they were not acquainted with in the first place. Theirs was a fearsome decision to make, which could either end in swift decimation or a longer wait for the inevitable.

This was love in all its glory and pain, like the type that Jesus exhibited when he left the confines of his comfort zone to enter into a place of rejection and hatred; yet he did it willingly to redeem and to reclaim for himself a lost people. This was faith; this was grace; this was the reality of the power of the gospel!

And it is this power that the apostle Paul wrote about in 1 Corinthians 1:18, *For the message of the cross is foolishness to those who are perishing, but to us who are being saved it is the power of God.* And, in the book of Romans, he writes, "For I am not ashamed of the gospel of Christ, for it is the POWER of God to salvation for EVERYONE who believes. . ."

May the Lord God, the Father of glory, truly enlighten the eyes of our hearts to know the hope to which he has called us, the riches of his glorious inheritance in the saints, and his incomparably great power for us who believe.

Athena D'Souza,
June, 2008.